Expressing Your Feelings

Roger T. Crenshaw, M.D.
P.O. Box 210278
Chula Vista, CA 91921

Lisa —
I hope that you
find my writing as useful
& fun as I did in the writing!

Roger T. Crenshaw M.D.
8.18.02

Printed in the United States of America

TABLE OF CONTENTS

PREFACE

The divorce rate continues to climb each year. Presently, more than 50 percent of marriages end in divorce. Masters and Johnson estimate that 50 to 60 percent of relationships experience sexual dysfunction. Arguments, conflict, lack of communication, and frustration are common in most marriages. In spite of these unfavorable statistics, new relationships continue to form. Human beings, in search of intimacy, trust, and companionship, seek each other out, hoping to become happier.

What do these figures suggest? Are human beings emotional lemmings destined for disaster? We don't think so.

Individuals are raised without being taught to communicate, cooperate, or deal with relationship problems productively. Ironically, the more intensely two people care for one another, the more likely they are to experience stress in their relationship. Hurts are deeper, arguments scar more, and resentments flourish.

One of the greatest frustrations is being unable to get along on a day-to-day basis with someone you know you love. This workbook is intended for motivated, caring individuals in distress. It is also designed for sound relationships that would like to flourish and realize their full potential.

The purpose of this workbook is to develop a practical, workable method to reduce anger, minimize relationship stress, and increase pleasurable experiences within the relationship. Two people are often more different than alike. These differences do not usually need to cause arguments and friction, but can be one of the most valuable aspects of a relationship. If these differences are dealt with productively, they will enhance a relationship significantly more often than they will stress it.

INTRODUCTION

This workbook is designed to help you begin to communicate more effectively. After completing this text, further improvement and success will depend upon whether you continue to practice what you have learned here. Some of the methods and attitudes we teach may feel awkward at first, but with practice and experience you will feel more comfortable and natural with them.

What we want you to be able to do after completing this workbook is exercise self-responsibility in your everyday life. We want you to be able to examine your daily experiences and reactions to discover the scope, sequence, and intensity of your feelings. We hope you will be able to deal more constructively with anger. In expressing your feelings, desires, and thoughts, we want you to be able to use "I" language and avoid defensiveness. We want you to be able to recognize when those you love are vulnerable. We want, ultimately, for you to be able to express yourself as effectively and constructively as possible with those you care about.

There are eight chapters, each of which is designed to help you work toward improving your interpersonal communication. Below is a brief description of each chapter.

Exercising Self-Responsibility	Here you'll be learning what we mean by self-responsibility. This is a central concept.
Exploring the Scope of Feelings	In this chapter, you'll become aware of the vast number and variety of feelings you may experience in any given situation, but that you may not have recognized previously.
Identifying the Sequence of Feelings	In this chapter you'll learn how to identify as primary or secondary the feelings you explored in the previous chapter. You'll learn why expressing primary feelings tends to be more constructive.
Dealing with Anger	Here you'll learn about how feelings vary in intensity. You'll learn a strategy for dealing more constructively with anger.

Using "I" Language	This is a critically important chapter in which you will learn a "language" that will help you say things in a more accurate and constructive way.
Identifying Defensiveness	Here you'll be learning how to recognize when you are behaving defensively.
Identifying Vulnerability	In this chapter, you'll learn to recognize when you or your partner are being vulnerable.
Effective Personal Expression	In this final chapter, you'll be putting together the skills you have learned in the previous chapters. You will be able to distinguish between effective and ineffective expression. This will help you become more aware of your own communication habits and improve your ability to communicate effectively.

HOW TO USE THIS WORKBOOK

This is a learner controlled workbook. **You** control the speed at which you progress and, to some degree, how much you read. Here's how.

There are eight chapters and each is organized in basically the same way.

Each chapter begins with a title page.

Next you'll find the **INTRODUCTION** to the chapter which includes your goal. Both are very important, so read them carefully.

Following the introductory page you'll find the **DEFINITION**. It is boxed and is the most critical information in the chapter. Read it carefully. You will probably refer to it often. Following it is the **ELABORATION**, a more detailed explanation of the definition plus some other valuable information. Read all of it. It averages three pages.

Next come the **EXAMPLES**. They are introduced by a page like this...

...or like this. Be sure to read the directions.

For each chapter there are three to five examples. You don't have to read all of them. Read only as many as you think you need to meet the goal stated in the Introduction.

For each example or sample conversation there is a section called **COMMENTARY**. It presents remarks about the example designed to help you understand the fine points. Read the commentary only if you need it to clarify an example. You'll get a better feel for this as you go through the book.

In every chapter you'll have the opportunity to **PRACTICE** meeting your goal. This page will give you the directions for completing the practice. Read it carefully.

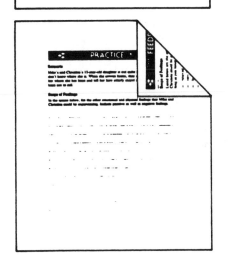

Some practice items take one page and some take two. Whichever is the case, you'll find the **FEED-BACK** or answer on the page(s) immediately following the item, except in Chapters Three and Four where there is no feedback. As with the examples, there is usually a **COMMENTARY** section included in the feedback for each practice item. It presents remarks about the item to help you understand the answers we provide in the feedback. Read it only if you need further explanation for a particular answer. Each chapter has four or five practice items. Do a couple of them and check the feedback after each. If you feel you've done well, go on to the next chapter. If you have any problems go back and review the definition, elaboration, and any examples you skipped the first time. Then try the rest of the practice.

Recommended Approach

To get the most out of *Expressing Your Feelings*, we recommend that you set aside some time each day for yourself — enough time that you can get through the book in one week. Read the first four chapters in the first two or three days. Don't discuss your feelings about what you've read with your partner until after you've read the chapters. Then complete the last four chapters in four days. The chapters average about 45 minutes in length. Try to do a whole chapter in one sitting — avoid stopping in the middle. We feel you will get the most out of this book by concentrating your efforts in this way.

IMPORTANT!

You may be tempted to just think through the practice items without writing your responses. However, the act of writing out your responses is critical to absorbing the material so that you can actually use the skills you learn. If you just read this book and don't respond actively, you will know more about communicating, but chances are, you won't actually be able to communicate better.

CHAPTER 1

EXERCISING SELF-RESPONSIBILITY

INTRODUCTION

PRESENTED IN this first chapter is one of the most important concepts in this workbook — the concept of self-responsibility. It is also one of the most difficult to accept because it is often confused with "selfishness." To exercise self-responsibility means to act in your own best interest. This may sometimes feel as though you are acting selfishly.

"Selfish" is a highly charged word in our society, as we are taught from childhood, "Don't be selfish," "Think of others first," "It's better to give than to receive," etc. Selfishness implies that you do what you want to without regard for anyone else's feelings.

It is true that to act consistently in your best interest may occasionally result in some distress for those you care about. But think about it this way. If you don't take care of yourself physically *and* mentally, if you become sick or severely depressed, how can you go on taking care of someone else? Instead, someone else will have to take care of you until you can function again in health and happiness. It is usually the case that when you are acting in your best interest to preserve your physical and psychological well-being, you are in a much better position to take care of those you love.

GOAL

We want you to be able to exercise self-responsibility in the course of your everyday life. In this chapter, you will take your first steps toward this goal. Given a scenario of an individual faced with a conflict and a description of his or her course of action, you'll be asked to determine if that individual is exercising self-responsibility.

You are exercising self-responsibility when you:

1. Act in your own best interest, having considered:

    a. Your wants and goals.

    b. The long- and short-term results of your actions.

    c. The possible effects of your actions on those you care about.

2. Communicate your intentions and feelings.

3. Do NOT blame others or hold them responsible for your behavior.

 ELABORATION

The concept of self-responsibility assumes that you are the world's authority on yourself and that you know better than anyone else what you want. Therefore, you are the only person who can make you happy. This means you must act in your own best interest. It also means that since you are the expert, you can't really hold someone else responsible for your behavior. Following is a more detailed explanation of each point in the definition.

1. Acting In Your Own Best Interest

Since you know more than anyone else about yourself, you are in the best position to achieve happiness and satisfaction for yourself. In order to act in your own best interest, you need to consider your desires and goals and the possible results of your actions. The more information you have about yourself, the situation, and the possible results for you and those you care for, the more responsibly you can choose your actions.

a. Knowing Your Wants and Goals

To decide what's best for your happiness, you need to know what you want. It's far more difficult to do what's best for yourself if you don't know what you want. If you are fully aware of your feelings, wants, and goals, you'll be prepared to make decisions affecting your happiness. We'll discuss this issue in more detail in Chapter Two.

b. Considering the Long- and Short-Term Results of Your Actions

Some individuals get the mistaken impression that exercising self-responsibility means doing whatever you want whenever you feel like it. For instance, if you work, you might decide you just don't feel like going in to work one day, or you don't like the project you're on, or you hate wearing a suit or a dress. It may or may not be in your best interest to skip work, stop work on the project, or wear jeans to the office. If you enjoy your work and your job is necessary to maintain a standard of living that you desire, it would not be in your best interest to jeopardize your job. If you do not basically enjoy your work, even if it is necessary to maintain your current standard of living, then it might be in your best interest to satisfy yourself by trying to change what you don't like and look for another alternative that better meets both your short-term and long-term needs.

In making sensible decisions about what is and isn't in your best interest, you need to consider the long- and short-term effects of your actions. If the immediate effect is pleasurable, but disruptive in the long run, that may affect your decision. It depends on what is important to you. It is critical that you identify what you really want and need and be prepared to do what is necessary to get what you want.

In the past, some therapists recommended that individuals focus on long-term goals. Now many therapists recommend focusing on the short-term goals only. Neither of these extremes is likely to help you achieve happiness. Your best interest will be served best by considering both the long- and short-term results in the light of what is most important to you.

c. Considering the Possible Effects of Your Actions on Those You Care About

It is in this aspect that self-responsibility is most often confused with selfishness. The exercise of self-responsibility does require that you do what's best for yourself, but it does NOT require that you ignore the feelings and desires of others. You need to consider the feelings of others for two reasons.

One reason is that in making any kind of important decision, you need to consider all of the facts and issues relevant to the decision. The way your partner feels is one of those issues. The more information you have about his or her feelings, the more likely you are to make a sensible and self-responsible decision.

The second reason to consider those you care about is that hurting people you love often hurts you and makes you unhappy. Making yourself unhappy is undesirable, and so is hurting someone you love. It is true, though, that on some occasions you will find that in order to act in your own best interest, someone you love will be hurt to some degree.

Active and Passive Exercise of Self-Responsibility

Self-responsibility can be exercised actively or passively. Often you will be taking some sort of action to achieve happiness or satisfaction. Sometimes, though, you'll just be letting things happen because you have decided they are pleasing to you. For example, if a man carries his partner off to the bedroom after announcing that he's going to make love to her, she can take no action and go along with it because she's decided that she likes what's happening. If, on the other hand, she does not want to make love and takes no action for fear of hurting his feelings, she is not exercising self-responsibility.

2. Communicating Your Intentions and Feelings

Too often the absence of communication results in defensiveness, misunderstanding, and hurt feelings. Because of this it is essential that whatever you decide to "do," you communicate your intentions to your partner and others you care about. If you are open about your feelings and intentions, your partner is much better prepared to deal with your actions and is less likely to be hurt by them.

3. Not Blaming Others or Holding Them Responsible for Your Behavior

When you hold others responsible for your happiness, you're hoping they will guess right about your wants and goals. When they fail to guess correctly and unhappiness results, you may make assumptions about their motives. For example, a man may feel sexually aroused and make subtle advances toward his partner. If she doesn't catch on, he may assume that she doesn't care about his needs or that she's rejecting his advances. Based on these assumptions, he'll probably blame her for his sexual frustration. You can see that this is not going to lead to anything constructive. In reality, his partner may not have noticed his advances. The fact is that people usually do the best they can with what they know. They cannot accurately read the feelings and thoughts of others. It is inevitable that situations like the one described above will occur, but blame is inappropriate between partners. It is assumed that if either of you *could* have done better, you would have. The following is a good analogy of this. Suppose your partner steps on your foot inadvertently. You would, of course, assume that your partner was unaware of hurting you. You would let him or her know and you would assume that he or she would move the offending foot... unless the other leg was broken. In the same way, your partner may hurt you unwittingly because something is distracting or upsetting him or her or because he or she is operating without important information from you. You will probably find yourself much happier if, when you feel wounded by your partner, you assume the hurt was unintentional and brought about by a lack of knowledge. You can minimize the chances of being hurt by keeping your loved ones well-informed. Don't expect them to guess. Tell them how you feel and what you want.

Of course, you could be mistaken about what you want and act in some way that does *not* increase your happiness. But *your* chances of being right about yourself are much greater than anyone else's.

If you're *not* happy or if you're dissatisfied with the results of your behavior, no one else is to blame. This does not mean you should blame yourself. Whether it's directed at yourself or at someone else, blame is *not* constructive. What self-responsibility does mean is that you are responsible for acting to make yourself happier. Under normal circumstances (nonviolent), no one can really force you to do anything. So if your behavior or overall happiness is displeasing to you, you must take responsibility for that and see that it does not continue.

Your best chance for achieving happiness and self-fulfillment is to rely on your self-knowledge and act in *your* best interest. Determine what your desires and goals are and take the responsibility for achieving them. Don't rely on others to help you out and avoid sacrificing your wants to make someone else happy, since the end product of such sacrifice is usually resentment. Just as you are responsible for your happiness, others are responsible for their own happiness.

The Role of Value Systems

We realize that a normal part of a person's psychological makeup is his or her value system. The development of self-responsibility includes being responsible for doing what you feel comfortable doing.

Your value system can have a great deal to do with what you will be comfortable with. In a given situation, you may decide to do something differently from someone else because of differences in your value systems; and still, both of you may be acting responsibly for yourselves.

For example, one individual may be having difficulties in his marriage and may have given what he believes to be as much as he can to the relationship. For this person, acting in his own best interest may lead to a decision to terminate the relationship. Another individual may be willing to give more to the relationship — either because he has a lower pain threshold, or because he has a value system which motivates him to make more of a commitment to the relationship.

The critical thing here is that each of us must evaluate our feelings and determine what we believe is best for us over both the short- and long-term. Only by considering our own feelings, not what someone else believes, will we be able to take responsibility for ourselves.

In the examples that follow, we will present what one person decided or considered. For that person, what was decided or considered will be responsible alternatives. As you read the examples, you may conclude that you would never consider doing what the person in the example did. We understand that this could be the case.

In any of the examples, we are not suggesting what *should* be decided. Rather, we are suggesting what might be considered. We are also proposing a rationale for why that consideration is a responsible one for the person in the example. This book does not attempt to portray in its examples any single value system. It does attempt to encourage people who are in conflict or who are having communication problems to consider both long- and short-term effects of their behavior in the light of their own value system.

EXAMPLES

THIS SECTION contains five examples. For each, a scenario will be presented describing a couple in a conflict situation. Following the scenario, two courses of action will be described. In each, one partner's reaction to the situation will be detailed. Course of Action A, described on the left, will show the individual *not* exercising self-responsibility. The same individual *will* exercise self-responsibility in Course of Action B on the right. Beneath each course of action is a commentary explaining how the individual is or is not exercising self-responsibility. We suggest that you read the scenario and then compare the courses of action. Read the commentaries only if you want to or if you need help understanding how the individual is or is not exercising self-responsibility. Study only as many examples as you need to be able to identify when an individual is exercising self-responsibility.

NOTE:

We would like to point out that, ideally, you need to evaluate your own behavior and not anyone else's. We are evaluating other individuals in the examples and practice items in this chapter in order to illustrate and teach the concept of self-responsibility. Outside of these materials, we would like to discourage judgment of other people's behavior. We suggest that you use your own actions as examples.

EXAMPLE 1

Scenario

Art is a very punctual person, but Lisa is chronically late. Whenever they try to go somewhere together, there is a conflict of wants. He wants to be on time. She is not nearly as concerned about punctuality.

Course of Action A

Art usually tries to hurry Lisa, but this only irritates her. He gets more and more frustrated as time goes on, and they often end up in an argument that causes them to be even later. The evening is often unpleasant.

COMMENTARY

Art is **not** exercising self-responsibility.

- Art is not acting in his best interest because he doesn't consider the short-term effect of trying to hurry Lisa — she gets irritated and they end up arguing.

- He hasn't clearly communicated his desires.

- Art is holding Lisa responsible for making him late.

Course of Action B

Art decides to take some precautions to prevent anxiety. When he feels that punctuality is crucial, he arranges for them to go separately. Other times he accepts being late and is content rather than getting angry. He discusses all this with Lisa and asks if there's any way he can help her be on time for his own sake.

COMMENTARY

Art **is** exercising self-responsibility.

- Art is acting in his best interest by arranging to be on time when it's important to him. He's considering Lisa's feelings by arranging for her transportation as well.

- He communicates his intentions to Lisa.

- He stops blaming her for their being late.

EXAMPLE 2

Scenario

Tom and Martha have been together for about ten years. Lately, Tom has been under a lot of stress from his job and their sex life has suffered. Tom is preoccupied much of the time and often depressed. First he began to lose his erection during sex. Now he has stopped approaching Martha sexually altogether.

Course of Action A

Martha tries everything she can think of to interest him in sex. She buys frilly nightgowns and arranges candlelight dinners. Nothing seems to help, and she feels hurt and frustrated. She's convinced that Tom is either seeing someone else or that he no longer finds her sexually attractive. She blames him for her frustration and begins pressuring him to prove that he still loves her.

Course of Action B

Martha discusses her feelings and fears with Tom and asks for feedback. She recognizes that her sexual frustration is a product of not having any sexual activity for a significant period of time. Tom tells her that he is having problems in other areas, and is **not** rejecting her personally. She asks if there is any way for her to help. In the meantime, to determine what is in her best interest, she considers the alternatives for relieving her sexual tensions: trying to get Tom more interested, distracting herself with cold showers, finding a lover, masturbating, etc.

COMMENTARY

Martha is **not** exercising self-responsibility.

● Martha is not acting in her best interest because she has not considered the long-term result of pressuring Tom to prove himself. She has not really considered his feelings.

● She has not communicated her needs very well before taking action.

● She blames Tom for her frustration and holds him responsible for making her feel better.

COMMENTARY

Martha **is** exercising self-responsibility.

● Martha is acting in her best interest because she has taken both the short- and the long-term results into account before acting. She asked Tom to discuss his feelings and has considered them carefully. Her actions will probably result in her getting some degree of sexual satisfaction without Tom's help.

● She communicates her desires to Tom and tells him how she plans to handle the situation.

● She stops blaming Tom for her frustration and assumes responsibility for taking care of it herself.

EXAMPLE 3

Scenario

Ellen and David are in their early thirties and have been together for about ten years. They have two children. Ellen is a housewife with no outside job. David is a sales manager for a nationwide corporation. At this point in his career he is concentrating on moving up the ladder in his company. Consequently, he travels a lot and attends many meetings and social engagements when he is at home. Often, Ellen is not included in the social engagements. More and more she is feeling the pressure of being solely responsible for the children and the house. Her own desire for social interaction is not being met.

Course of Action A

Ellen decides that she must sacrifice her needs at this point so David can further his career. She immerses herself in the tasks of child-rearing and taking care of the house. She attempts to find things to substitute for her desire to socialize. She pledges her support to David but becomes resentful when he doesn't seem to appreciate it. He is rarely home, but when he is, she finds it difficult to interact with him pleasantly because she resents him for not fulfilling her needs.

COMMENTARY

Ellen is **not** exercising self-responsibility.

- Ellen is not acting in her best interest. Instead, she is committing herself to acting in David's and her children's best interests. She's ignoring the short-term frustration and unhappiness that this is causing her.

- She has not clearly communicated her desires or intentions to him. In this case, she's expecting him to **know** how much she's sacrificing for him.

- She's blaming him for not appreciating her and for not fulfilling her desires.

Course of Action B

Ellen realizes that David is pursuing a goal that is very important to him, but at the same time she is determined to fulfill her own wants. She wants to socialize and interact with friends — so when invited to parties, she accepts with or without David. She leaves the children with a babysitter more often so she can get away from the house. She discusses her plans with David and tells him that she is no longer going to attend to all the household business, and if he doesn't want to take care of it, she intends to hire an accountant or business manager. At the same time, she is examining the relationship she has with David to determine whether it is in her best interest for them to stay together.

COMMENTARY

Ellen is exercising self-responsibility.

- Ellen is acting in her best interest because she is considering both the long- and short-term results of her actions.

- She communicates her feelings and plans to David.

- She stops blaming him for her unhappiness and assumes responsibility for making herself happier.

12

EXAMPLE 4

Scenario

Fred and Mary have recently bought the dream house for which they've been planning and saving for five years. From the time they moved in (February) until September, they spent every weekend working together on the house and the yard. Now that football season has started, Fred has stopped working on the house and spends every weekend watching football on TV. Mary is getting irritated and frustrated at the state of the yard, but Fred just isn't as interested in doing yard work as he once was.

Course of Action A

Mary begins to prod Fred more and more about his responsibilities to the house. The more she prods and the less response she gets, the angrier she becomes. She accuses him of not living up to his responsibilities and of jeopardizing their investment. In addition, she is wearing herself out trying to do all the housework, yardwork, and make improvements on the home as well.

COMMENTARY

Mary is **not** exercising self-responsibility.

- She is not acting in her best interest because she hasn't carefully considered the short-term results of her actions — she is exhausted and frustrated. In addition, she has not considered Fred's feelings. She doesn't even know what they are.

- Rather than communicating her desires and intentions clearly, she nags Fred about his responsibilities.

- She is blaming Fred for her dissatisfaction and holding him responsible for "making things right."

Course of Action B

Mary expresses her concerns to Fred, and he tells her that right now his primary interest on weekends is watching football. She accepts the problem as her own and starts figuring out ways that she can get housework, yardwork, and home improvements done without exhausting herself, such as hiring help. She tells Fred that she's going to try to get as much done as possible and accept what she can't achieve.

COMMENTARY

Mary **is** exercising self-responsibility.

- She is acting in her best interest because she has considered more carefully the long- and short-term results of her actions. She has taken Fred's feelings into account and has made her choice of action based on all this information.

- She expresses her desires more clearly and tells Fred what she's going to do.

- She stops blaming Fred and accepts the problem as her own. She assumes responsibility for taking care of it herself.

EXAMPLE 5

Scenario

Bob wants to fly to Utah to hunt deer for five days with some friends. During his trip, his and Judy's anniversary will occur, and Judy is very anxious that he be home to celebrate. He suggests that she come on the hunting trip, but she is not interested in hunting or camping. She tells Bob it is really very important to her that they celebrate their anniversary together. He explains that the hunting trip is important to him because it's the only one planned for the year.

Course of Action A

Bob decides that he will go on the hunting trip and celebrate their anniversary when he returns. While on the trip, Bob begins to feel guilty about disappointing Judy. Thinking about how upset she might be when he returns eventually ruins the expedition for him. He goes home feeling resentful toward her for taking the enjoyment out of the week.

COMMENTARY

Bob is **not** exercising self-responsibility.

- Bob is not acting in his best interest because he did not take into account the long-term result of his action, i.e., that he would feel guilty about going.

- He doesn't communicate to Judy his desire to celebrate when he gets back.

- Bob then blames Judy for his not enjoying himself.

Course of Action B

Bob decides to go on the hunting trip even though he knows Judy will be very disappointed. He tells her that he will be glad to have a special celebration when he comes back because their anniversary is important to him, too. Knowing that Judy is still rather upset about the trip, he goes and has a good time. When he returns, he makes the offer again of a late, but special, celebration.

COMMENTARY

Bob is exercising self-responsibility.

- Bob is acting in his best interest because he does consider Judy's desires, and he does think about the long-term results before making his decision. He tries to satisfy his desires as well as hers.

- Bob tells Judy about his plans and his desire to celebrate when he returns.

- Bob then has a good time and does not blame Judy for her feelings.

PRACTICE

THIS SECTION presents four scenarios. Following each is a description of the course of action taken by one of the individuals involved. You are to determine if, in your opinion, the individual is exercising self-responsibility. Once you have made your choice and written YES or NO in the blank provided, you are to state your reasons for making that choice. In other words, if you said YES, tell why you think the individual is exercising self-responsibility. If you said NO, tell why the individual is *not* exercising self-responsibility. Your remarks need not be lengthy or detailed.

After completing each practice scenario, study the feedback on the following page before going to the next item. Your YES/NO response is correct if it matches the response given in the feedback. However, your explanation may be a little different. If, after doing the first two, you feel you are doing well, skip to Item 5, and then go on to the next chapter. If you have any trouble with the practice, go back and review the definition, the elaboration, and the examples.

Item 5 is a bit different, and you'll find directions about how to do it when you get to it.

PRACTICE 1

Scenario

Ralph invites Emily to a baseball game one Saturday afternoon. Having never been to a baseball game at a stadium, Emily doesn't know if she would enjoy it or not. She decides to go and find out.

Course of Action

While at the game, Emily decides she is bored and uncomfortable, and she wishes she hadn't come. She sits through the game feeling very frustrated because she wants to go home and the game seems endless. By the end of the game she is angry and resentful that Ralph didn't sense she wasn't enjoying herself. She blames him for her wasting her afternoon.

Is Emily exercising self-responsibility? _____
Yes/No

How is Emily exercising/**not** exercising self-responsibility?

_____

_____

_____

_____

_____

REMINDER

Did you remember to write your answer? If not, we'd like to emphasize again how important it is that you do. Not only will it help you focus your attention on what you're learning but getting it down on paper will help you evaluate it more objectively. If you don't want to write in the book, write on scratch paper. Also, you don't have to write as though you were writing for an English composition class. Just get your ideas and answers down in a way you are most comfortable with.

Is Emily exercising self-responsibility? _____NO_____

How is Emily **not** exercising self-responsibility?

- She is not acting in her best interest because she isn't considering either the short- or long-term results of getting angry. In addition, she's not really thinking about what she wants, which is to go home.

- She hasn't communicated her desires to Ralph and is expecting him to know them anyway.

- She's blaming Ralph for her discomfort and for not paying attention to her desires.

Scenario

Grace has been married for 25 years and, for the most part, the union has been a disaster in her eyes. She gave up a modest career to be married and have a family. The last of her children moved out several years ago, and since then Grace's dissatisfaction with her marriage has steadily increased.

Course of Action

Grace realizes that although her 25-year marriage may have been a mistake, it was her choice to get married and to stay married for 25 years. She begins to examine her present desires and goals to discover what changes need to be made for her to become happier. She talks with her husband about her feelings and asks for his help in finding a solution.

Is Grace exercising self-responsibility? _____
                                              Yes/No

How is Grace exercising/**not** exercising self-responsibility?

_____

_____

_____

_____

_____

_____

FEEDBACK 2

Is Grace exercising self-responsibility? _____YES_____

How is Grace exercising/**not** exercising self-responsibility?

- She is acting in her best interest by carefully examining what she wants, so she can become happier now and in the long run. She's considering her husband's feelings by asking for his input.

- She communicates her feelings to him.

- She does **not** blame him for her present situation or her past unhappiness.

Scenario

Robert has just been informed that a high school girl friend has moved to his city, and he decides that he would like to see her. Nancy is extremely jealous and tells Robert she would rather he didn't make the visit.

Course of Action

Robert decides that he would still like to see his former girl friend. He explains to Nancy that, while he loves her, he still has some feelings for his friend, and he's curious as to what she's been up to for the last six years. He tells Nancy that he can understand her concern and invites her to come along with him.

Is Robert exercising self-responsibility? _____
Yes/No

How is Robert exercising/**not** exercising self-responsibility?

_____

_____

_____

_____

_____

_____

21

Is Robert exercising self-responsibility?   __YES__

How is Robert exercising/**not** exercising self-responsibility?

- He is acting in his best interest because he has considered his wants, i.e., visiting his friend, the long- and short-term effects of his action, and the effects of his action on his relationship with Nancy.

- He has communicated his intentions and feelings to Nancy.

- He hasn't blamed Nancy for being jealous. In the best interest of his relationship with Nancy, he has suggested that she be included in the experience.

PRACTICE 4

Scenario

Barbara and Henry have received an invitation to a party given by a friend of Barbara's. Henry doesn't know Barbara's friend or anybody who will be at the party and is reluctant to go. Barbara is very eager to attend, but is uncomfortable about going by herself, so she tries very hard to persuade Henry to go.

Course of Action

Henry decides that he feels very strongly about not going to the party and tells Barbara so. He also tells her he doesn't mind if she goes by herself. She is very aggravated with him and goes to the party without saying good-bye. Henry feels sorry that he had to disappoint her, but spends an enjoyable evening alone.

Is Henry exercising self-responsibility?   _____
                                               Yes/No

How is Henry exercising/**not** exercising self-responsibility?

_____

_____

_____

_____

_____

_____

FEEDBACK 4

Is Henry exercising self-responsibility? _____ YES _____

How is Henry exercising/**not** exercising self-responsibility?

- He is acting in his best interest because he has considered both the long- and short-term results of going to the party. He's considered Barbara's desires; even though he's decided not to go, he assures her that he doesn't mind her going.

- He communicates his desires and intentions to Barbara.

- Henry does not blame Barbara for being aggravated with him and enjoys his evening.

PRACTICE 5

Given the scenario you just read for Practice 4, we're going to ask you to describe a course of action in which Barbara is exercising more self-responsibility.

In exercising self-responsibility, Barbara will:

1. Act in her best interest, having considered:

    a. Her wants and goals.

    b. The long- and short-term effects of her actions.

    c. The possible effects of her actions on Henry.

2. Communicate her feelings and intentions to Henry.

3. Not blame Henry or hold him responsible for her feelings or behavior.

Use the rest of this page to write your answer. Since you don't know Barbara, you may find it easier to imagine yourself in her place and describe how you would respond. Be as thorough as you can.

_____

_____

_____

_____

_____

_____

_____

_____

_____

_____

To find out how well you responded, use the checklist we've provided below. If you mark any of the questions "No," you may want to go back and add to your description.

	Yes	No
1. Did you describe Barbara acting in her best interest? (Your answer will be "Yes" if the answers for a, b, and c, are "Yes.")	☐	☐
a. Did you describe Barbara examining what her wants and goals are and acting in accordance with them?	☐	☐
b. Did you describe Barbara considering the long- and short-term results of her actions?	☐	☐
c. Did you describe Barbara considering Henry's feelings?	☐	☐
2. Did you describe Barbara communicating her feelings and intentions to Henry?	☐	☐
3. Did you describe Barbara as NOT blaming Henry or holding him responsible?	☐	☐

CHAPTER 2

EXPLORING THE SCOPE OF FEELINGS

INTRODUCTION

TOO OFTEN individuals prevent themselves from exercising self-responsibility because they act before they are aware of everything they feel. In other words they're acting without critically important information about themselves. In any situation or experience, it is important to be aware of the entire range of your feelings, not just the most immediate and most powerful of them. Very often you will find that your complete awareness of how you feel will lead you to behave quite differently than if you acted on your immediate impulses. It stands to reason that if there are other feelings beneath those impulses, you'll want to know about them.

GOAL

We want you to be able to examine your reactions to experiences and discover the scope of your feelings so you can act self-responsibly. In this chapter, you will take the first steps toward this goal. Given a situation, you'll be asked to place yourself in the situation and imagine what your own feelings would be. It's not so important that you list the same feelings we do as it is that you become aware of the vast scope of feelings possible in any situation.

DEFINITION

A feeling is an emotional or physical reaction to an experience. The scope of feeling in any situation is *all* of the emotional and physical reactions experienced by the individual.

ELABORATION

Emotional and Physical Feelings

Feelings are reactions to experiences. These reactions can be emotional and physical. For example, suppose you've had a very bad day; nothing has gone the way you planned. Physically, your reactions may be fatigue, headache, and generalized tension. Emotionally, you may feel frustrated, irritable, or depressed. Every day of your life you will experience physical and emotional reactions to things going on around you and inside of you.

The Scope of Emotional and Physical Reactions

In most situations, you are likely to experience more than one feeling at the same time. Often, it may seem that there is only one powerful emotion. But if you look deeper, you are likely to find that your feelings are more complex than you first realized. They may even contradict each other. For example, suppose your partner spends a lot of time at a party talking to an attractive member of the opposite sex. Your most powerful feeling might be jealousy. If you assume that jealousy is the only feeling you have, you're probably not in touch with everything you feel. You may feel hurt that your partner seems to be choosing someone other than you to talk to. You may be *fearful* that an intimate relationship might develop. On the other hand, a part of you may feel *pleased* that your partner is having a good time. You may feel *freer* to wander around and talk to whomever you like. As you can see, some of these feelings are contradictory, but it is important to be aware of their existence. If you assume that jealousy is your only reaction, you are likely to behave quite differently than if you are aware of the full range of your feelings.

Censoring or Judging Feelings

Censoring and judging feelings are *not* constructive activities, and here are some reasons why:

1. Feelings are facts and as facts are not good or bad. It is usually easier for individuals to accept that physical feelings are facts. A headache or a sore throat is accepted as a fact. People don't typically think of themselves as good or bad because they have a physical ailment. They may try to ignore it to some degree, but they don't usually behave as though it didn't exist. Physical feelings give us information about our bodies. In the same way, emotional feelings tell us about our psychological condition and it is not constructive to censor or judge them.

   For example, many people believe jealousy is a "bad" feeling. But if you're feeling jealous, it's not going to do you any good to judge yourself as "bad." The feeling is a fact. It tells you something about where you are right now. You don't have to like it, but telling yourself that jealousy is bad won't make you stop feeling jealous — neither will trying to ignore it. In censoring feelings you may act without important information about yourself and, therefore, you may make an inappropriate decision for yourself without realizing it. If you are not aware of the full scope of your feelings, it is difficult to act in your best interest.

2. You are *not* responsible for your feelings. Even though you are responsible for your behavior, you cannot directly control your feelings. Your feelings are triggered by the current situation and the depth and nature of those feelings is based on your previous experience which is personal and unique to you. Feelings are based more on your preceding experience than on the current trigger itself. Suppose, for example, that a woman has grown up with an alcoholic father who became violent when drunk. Her partner is normally a moderate drinker, but one evening he gets drunk at a party. When they get home, she locks herself in their room for the night and the next day she hardly speaks to him. Her feelings of fear, hurt, resentment, and anger are triggered more by her experiences with her father than by what actually happened. Another individual with different experiences would probably have felt and reacted quite differently. Because emotional reactions reflect each individual's unique experience, they are not subject to question or criticism. Asking why or judging feelings as good or bad is destructive and pointless. It creates anxiety and wastes emotional energy. Since feelings are facts and since you have no direct control over them, it is wisest to take them at face value as useful information about yourself.

There are hundreds of words to express or describe feelings. In this book we'll be using only a fraction of them. The following "Vocabulary of Feelings" presents a great variety and number of words used to describe feelings. You may want to study the list and use it to help you expand your own vocabulary so you can speak about your feelings more specifically.

THE VOCABULARY OF FEELINGS[1]

Levels of Intensity	Happy	Caring	Depressed	Inadequate	Fearful
Strong	thrilled	tenderness toward	desolate	worthless	terrified
	on cloud nine	affection for	dejected	good for nothing	frightened
	ecstatic	captivated by	hopeless	washed up	intimidated
	overjoyed	attached to	alienated	powerless	horrified
	excited	devoted to	depressed	helpless	desperate
	elated	adoration	gloomy	impotent	panicky
	sensational	loving	dismal	crippled	terror-stricken
	exhilarated	infatuated	bleak	inferior	stage fright
	fantastic	enamored	in despair	emasculated	dread
	terrific	cherish	empty	useless	vulnerable
	on top of the world	idolize	barren	finished	paralyzed
	turned on	worship	grieved	like a failure	
	euphoric		grief		
	enthusiastic		despair		
	delighted		grim		
	marvelous				
	great				
Moderate	cheerful	caring	distressed	inadequate	afraid
	light-hearted	fond of	upset	whipped	scared
	happy	regard	downcast	defeated	fearful
	serene	respectful	sorrowful	incompetent	apprehensive
	wonderful	admiration	demoralized	inept	jumpy
	up	concern for	discouraged	overwhelmed	shaky
	aglow	hold dear	miserable	ineffective	threatened
	glowing	prize	pessimistic	lacking	distrustful
	in high spirits	taken with	tearful	deficient	risky
	jovial	turned on	weepy	unable	alarmed
	riding high	trust	rotten	incapable	butterflies
	elevated	close	awful	small	awkward
	neat		horrible	insignificant	defensive
			terrible	like Casper Milquetoast	
			blue	unfit	
			lost	unimportant	
			melancholy	incomplete	
				no good	
				immobilized	
Mild	glad	warm toward	unhappy	lacking confidence	nervous
	good	friendly	down	unsure of yourself	anxious
	contented	like	low	uncertain	unsure
	satisfied	positive toward	bad	weak	hesitant
	gratified		blah	inefficient	timid
	pleasant		disappointed		shy
	pleased		sad		worried
	fine		glum		uneasy
					bashful
					embarrassed
					ill at ease
					doubtful
					jittery
					on edge
					uncomfortable
					self-conscious

Levels of Intensity	Confused	Hurt	Angry	Lonely	Guilt-Shame
Strong	bewildered puzzled baffled perplexed trapped confounded in a dilemma befuddled in a quandary full of questions confused	crushed destroyed ruined degraded pain(ed) wounded devastated tortured disgraced humiliated at the mercy of cast off forsaken rejected discarded	furious enraged seething outraged infuriated burned up pissed off fighting mad nauseated violent indignant hatred bitter galled vengeful hateful vicious	isolated abandoned all alone forsaken cut off	sick at heart unforgivable humiliated disgraced degraded horrible mortified exposed
Moderate	mixed-up disorganized foggy troubled adrift lost at loose ends going around in circles disconcerned frustrated flustered in a bind ambivalent disturbed helpless embroiled	hurt belittled shot down overlooked abused depreciated criticized censured discredited laughed at mistreated ridiculed devalued scorned mocked scoffed at used exploited slammed slandered cheapened	resentful irritated hostile annoyed upset with agitated mad aggravated offended antagonistic exasperated belligerent mean vexed spiteful vindictive	lonely alienated estranged remote alone apart from others insulated from others	ashamed guilty remorseful crummy to blame lost face demeaned
Mild	uncertain unsure bothered uncomfortable undecided	put down neglected overlooked minimized let down unappreciated taken for granted	uptight disgusted bugged turned off put out miffed irked perturbed ticked off teed off chagrined cross dismayed impatient	left out excluded lonesome distant aloof	regretful wrong embarrassed at fault in error responsible for blew it goofed lament

___

[1]Vocabulary of Feelings reprinted with permission of the publisher.

From: Hammond, D. Corydon, Hepworth, Dean H., and Smith, Veon G. Improving Therapeutic Communication: A Guide for Developing Effective Techniques. San Francisco: Jossey-Bass, 1977.

3. Another important point is that since *you* are not responsible for your feelings, neither is anyone else. No one can be blamed for the way you feel about something. This is a difficult point for most people to understand and accept, but look at it this way: Since your feelings are a product of a current event coupled with all of your preceding experience, it is extremely difficult for someone else to accurately predict how you will feel about something. You have probably found it difficult to predict your own feelings. Since it is almost impossible for someone else to know exactly how you will feel about something, that person cannot be held responsible for your feelings.

4. Acceptance of your feelings means more than not censoring, judging, or analyzing them. Acceptance means that you acknowledge your feelings as facts and realities. It doesn't mean you have to *like* all of your feelings. You can accept the fact that you are fat without liking it. Once you accept it as a reality though, you are better able to begin doing something about it. If, instead of accepting your weight, you condemn yourself for being ugly, inadequate, or weak, you're more likely to choose a course of action that is not in your best interest, like eating a box of chocolates.

   Positive feelings can also be difficult to accept. When you are extremely happy, you may be tempted to ask yourself questions like, "How long can this last?" or "When will it end?" Accepting the feeling without judging or analyzing it will usually help positive feelings last longer. The minute you worry that you won't be happy forever, you are no longer as happy as you were a moment ago. Accept happy feelings and enjoy them.

   It is equally important to accept the feelings of others, whether you like those feelings or not, and even if they hurt you deeply. Those feelings are as factual and real as your own and need to be accepted as such.

EXAMPLES

THIS SECTION contains four examples. For each example, there is a scenario that begins to describe a situation and the most powerful reaction experienced by the individual. Following the scenario, a further description is given as to the feelings the individual might be experiencing. This section is titled "Scope of Feelings," and the physical and emotional reactions are listed. The order is of no particular importance. The commentary at the bottom of the page provides some useful comments about the scenario and the feelings elicited. Study only as many examples as you need to be able to list the various reactions an individual might have to a particular situation or experience.

NOTE:

As in the previous chapter, we are using other individuals as examples to demonstrate the definition. Outside of this text, we recommend that you do not go around second-guessing other people's feelings. Put yourself into the situation or experience and imagine what your *own* feelings would be.

EXAMPLE 1

Scenario

Anna's youngest son has just left for college and won't be home again until Christmas vacation. There are no younger children, and the older kids all live out of town. Anna's most powerful reaction when her son leaves is depression.

Scope of Feelings

In the days after her son's departure, Anna looks more closely at her feelings and finds them to be somewhat complex. She feels:

— lonely because she now spends most of the day all by herself.

— worried about her son's health and well-being.

— regretful of any arguments they had in the past year.

— appreciative of his personality because she misses him.

— excited for him because he's starting his own life of independence.

— relieved that she doesn't have to pick up after him all the time.

— tired from the pressure that steadily built up until his actual departure.

— nostalgic about her own days in college.

COMMENTARY

Included above are:

— physical feelings: fatigue.
— positive emotional feelings: appreciation, excitement, relief.
— negative emotional feelings: loneliness, worry, regret.

EXAMPLE 2

Scenario

Howard buys Janice a new refrigerator for Christmas. She thanks him for his thoughtful gift but later tells him it isn't the color she had wanted and it doesn't have an icemaker. Howard's initial reaction is anger. He tells Janice to return the refrigerator herself and that he doesn't care what she does.

Scope of Feelings

After calming down, Howard examines his feelings more closely and finds that he also feels:

— hurt that she hadn't entirely liked the refrigerator he chose.

— frustrated that he had gone to so much trouble to get something that wasn't quite right.

— fearful that the present model could not be exchanged or that the new model might be significantly more expensive.

— glad that she told him what she really wants because he wants her to have it.

— fearful that he'll have to go to a lot of trouble to exchange the refrigerator.

— irritated that she couldn't be satisfied with it as it was.

— insecure because she might see him as unable to do anything right.

— hopeful that they can get a refrigerator with an icemaker after all, because that's what he really wants too, even though it seems economically impractical.

— unhappy that he can't provide her with all the things she would like to have.

COMMENTARY

Included above are:

— positive emotional feelings: gladness, hope.
— negative emotional feelings: hurt, frustration, fear, unhappiness, insecurity.

EXAMPLE 3

Scenario

Chuck is setting up a new business and, consequently, works late hours and weekends. One particular weekend, Chuck has some free time. He decides to spend it with his two children. The youngest is in Little League, and Chuck wants to help him practice batting. The older child is a teenager, and Chuck wants to take her shopping for a stereo that she's been saving for. These activities with his children will probably exhaust Chuck's free time for the weekend. Betty's initial reaction is jealousy because it seems he is choosing the children over her.

Scope of Feelings

Examining her feelings more deeply, Betty finds that she also feels:

— guilty about her jealousy of her children.

— happy that he cares for his children enough to take time for them.

— proud that he is practicing with his young son.

— angry because he isn't taking time to spend with her.

— physically tired due to the burden of making almost all decisions herself.

— fearful that when the kids grow up and move away he won't ever take time for her.

— thankful that Chuck, busy as he is, takes more time for his children than her father did for her.

— resentful that she gets all the drudgery and he gets to have fun with the children.

— fearful that the children will like him more than her.

COMMENTARY

Included above are:

— physical feelings: fatigue.

— positive emotional feelings: happiness, pride, thankfulness.

— negative emotional feelings: guilt, anger, fear, jealousy, resentment.

EXAMPLE 4

Scenario

After eighteen years with Tony, Karen is finding time to indulge in her artistic hobbies. She becomes quite good in a very short time and starts having her own shows and selling her artwork at respectable prices. Tony is a physician who worked his way through medical school and worked hard at building a strong and profitable practice. He vacillates between two very powerful reactions. He feels extremely proud of her talents and accomplishments. At other times he's resentful and grumbles about how much it's costing him tax-wise to support her business.

Scope of Feelings

Thinking about it more, Tony realizes that he also feels:

— resentful that it's been so much easier for her than it was for him.
— resentful because she can work at home and when she feels like it, while he must work many hours day and night at his office and the hospital.
— left out because he can't really participate in her work.
— uncomfortable around the friends she's met as an artist.
— fearful that she will become more prominent than he.
— fearful that she will meet interesting people and become bored with him.
— left out because she is busy with her career and no longer waits on him as much as she used to.
— very loving toward her because she is growing as a person and becoming more and more interesting and confident in herself.
— anxious for her to do well and succeed for her sake.
— insecure because she no longer depends on him the way she used to.
— nostalgic about the sense of emotional security he used to have.
— proud of her achievements and ability.
— worried that she might not be able to handle her success or failure.

COMMENTARY

Included above are:

— positive emotional feelings: love, pride.
— negative emotional feelings: resentment, fear, feeling of being left out, discomfort, anxiety, worry, insecurity.

PRACTICE

FOLLOWING ARE five practice items. For each there is a scenario that briefly describes a situation. You are to describe the scope of feelings that the person involved might be experiencing. Include positive, negative, emotional, and physical feelings. Feel free to interpret the situation as imaginatively as you wish. You may find it especially helpful to use your own feelings in a similar situation as a guide.

On the page following the practice item is the feedback for the item. In the feedback, we list the feelings we came up with. If you came up with a different list, your answer is not wrong. We'd like you to be able to list at least four feelings for each item, but list as many more than that as you can.

After completing each practice item, study the feedback. If you feel you've done the first couple well, go on to the next chapter. If you have any trouble with the practice, refer to the definition, elaboration, or examples for help. Then try the practice again.

PRACTICE 1

Scenario

Mike's and Christina's 15-year-old daughter is out quite late one night, and they don't know where she is. When she arrives home, they express anger. They ask her where she has been and tell her how utterly stupid and thoughtless she has been not to call.

Scope of Feelings

In the spaces below, list the other emotional and physical feelings that Mike and Christina could be experiencing. Include positive as well as negative feelings.

_____

_____

_____

_____

_____

_____

_____

_____

_____

_____

REMINDER

Don't forget to write your answers.

Scope of Feelings

Listed below are the other emotional and physical feelings we thought Mike and Christina could be experiencing. Your list may differ, but don't be concerned as long as you listed at least four reactions. They might be:

— relieved when she finally came home.

— very happy that nothing had happened to her.

— hurt because she hadn't called to let them know where she was.

— frustrated while she was gone because they didn't know whether to call around at her friends' houses and risk embarrassing her or to call the police.

— fearful while she was gone that something terrible had happened to her.

— irritated because they had asked her repeatedly to call when she was late.

— having headaches and stomach upset due to the intensity of their stress.

— physically tired due to the late hour and tense due to their anxiety.

— frustrated because this has happened several times and they don't know how to prevent it.

COMMENTARY

Included above are:

— physical feelings: fatigue, tenseness, headache, stomach upset.

— positive emotional feelings: relief, happiness.

— negative emotional feelings: fear, hurt, irritation, hysteria, frustration.

PRACTICE 2

Scenario

Don's father has suffered a number of strokes and now requires full-time care and treatment in a nursing home. Lately, his father's moods have been very unpredictable — some days pleasant and conversational and other days disoriented and abusive. The nursing home is quite expensive and the payments cut significantly into the family budget. One day, while Don is visiting him, his father is particularly abusive. Don becomes very angry and storms out vowing never to visit again and to let the state take over his father's support.

Scope of Feelings

In the spaces below, list the other emotional and physical feelings Don could be experiencing. Include positive as well as negative feelings.

_____

_____

_____

_____

_____

_____

_____

_____

_____

_____

_____

_____

Scope of Feelings

Listed below are the other emotional and physical feelings we thought Don could be experiencing. Your list may differ, but don't be concerned as long as you listed at least four reactions. Don might feel:

— resentful that the nursing home payments prevent him from spending as much as he'd like on his family.

— pleased that he can support his father financially now that he needs him, particularly since his father has helped him out frequently over the years.

— happy on the many days when his father is in good spirits and coherent.

— sad and depressed on the days when his father is incoherent or nasty.

— nostalgic about the many good times he remembers having with his dad when he was well.

— fearful of the day when his father will die.

— fearful that the same thing will happen to him when he reaches his fathers age.

COMMENTARY

Included above are:

— positive emotional feelings: happiness, pleasure.
— negative emotional feelings: resentment, sadness, depression, fear.

PRACTICE 3

Scenario

Richard and Laura receive a note from their son's school complaining of misbehavior on his part. Naturally, they are both disturbed. Richard becomes angry and blames Laura for being too lenient and not allowing him to discipline the boy more firmly.

Scope of Feelings

In the spaces below, list the other emotional and physical feelings that Richard could be experiencing. Include positive as well as negative feelings.

_____

_____

_____

_____

_____

_____

_____

_____

_____

_____

_____

_____

_____

_____

Scope of Feelings

Listed below are the other emotional and physical feelings we thought Richard could be experiencing. Your list may differ, but don't be concerned as long as you listed at least four reactions. Richard may feel:

— love for his child who is having trouble.

— fearful that his son's behavior will continue and cause trouble for him later in life.

— helpless because his son won't listen to him.

— frustrated because he doesn't know how to stop it.

— disappointed that the boy isn't living up to his expectations.

— guilty that maybe he hasn't spent enough time with the boy.

— amused because he remembers similar instances from his own childhood.

— somewhat proud of his son's spirit.

— hopeful that Laura is correct in her less strict approach because the problem isn't as serious as he sometimes feels it is.

— tired and irritable after a long day at work.

— depressed that he doesn't seem to be able to solve the problem.

— protective of his child because he feels the school system and the teachers are cold and indifferent.

COMMENTARY

Included above are:

— physical feelings: fatigue.

— positive emotional feelings: amusement, pride, love, hope, protectiveness.

— negative emotional feelings: worry, frustration, guilt, irritability, depression, helplessness.

Scenario

One evening when feeling affectionate, Ken reaches over to hug Peggy and then suggests intercourse. Her immediate reaction is to ask angrily why he can't be content with holding. She accuses him of not knowing how to be tender. She tells him that affection is never enough for him, that all he ever wants is sex. Ken's initial reaction is anger. He retorts, "The last thing I want is sex with a bitch like you."

Scope of Feelings

In the spaces below, list the other emotional and physical feelings that Ken could be experiencing. Include positive as well as negative feelings.

_____

_____

_____

_____

_____

_____

_____

_____

_____

_____

_____

FEEDBACK 4

Scope of Feelings

Listed below are the other emotional and physical feelings we thought Ken might be experiencing. Your list may differ, but don't be concerned as long as you listed at least four reactions. Ken might feel:

— rejected.
— hurt because Peggy thinks he's interested only in sex.
— hurt by the intensity of her reaction and the things she said.
— sexually frustrated because he's extremely aroused.
— fearful that the situation will continue.
— irritated because he thinks Peggy is being unfair in her judgment.
— fearful that she doesn't love him or find him sexually attractive.
— love for Peggy despite her reaction.

COMMENTARY

Included above are:

— physical feelings: sexual frustration.
— positive emotional feelings: love.
— negative emotional feelings: rejection, hurt, fear, irritability.

PRACTICE 5

Using the scenario from Practice 4, list the other emotional and physical feelings that *Peggy* could be experiencing in the space below. Include positive as well as negative feelings.

_____

_____

_____

_____

_____

_____

_____

_____

_____

_____

_____

_____

_____

_____

_____

_____

FEEDBACK 5

Scope of Feelings

Listed below are the other emotional and physical feelings we thought Peggy might be experiencing. Your list may differ, but don't be concerned as long as you listed at least four reactions. Peggy might feel:

— pressured to respond sexually.

— hurt that Ken can't love her "for herself."

— fear that she won't be able to please Ken.

— pleased that he wants her.

— upset that she rejected him.

— confused about why she rejected him.

— fear that he'll leave her if she continues to act this way.

— resentful of Ken for putting her in an uncomfortable position.

— love for Ken.

— tired after a long day.

— tense because Ken is upset with her.

COMMENTARY

Included above are:

— physical feelings: fatigue, tenseness.
— positive emotional feelings: pleasure, love.
— negative emotional feelings: pressure, hurt, fear, confusion, resentment.

CHAPTER 3

IDENTIFYING THE SEQUENCE OF FEELINGS

INTRODUCTION

I N THE previous chapter we discussed the broad scope of feelings we all experience and we presented some exercises that would help you identify your own feelings. In this chapter, we want to expand on this concept of feelings and discuss sequences of feelings—sequences that can, under certain circumstances, lead to feelings which are crippling or destructive in interpersonal relationships.

The most intense feeling a person has in a given situation is often not the first feeling experienced in that situation. It may, however, be the first feeling that registers (i.e., is noticed, responded to, etc.). As we discuss the sequences of feelings, you will find that we generally have to think carefully to identify the initial feeling in a sequence—whereas later feelings are often very obvious and often cause us to act.

The initial or *primary* feelings in the sequence can be the cause of later or *secondary* feelings. For example, the father who is angry with his son who has just returned home at 2 o'clock in the morning probably recognizes he is angry and will act upon that anger. But what caused the anger? The feelings preceding his anger (his primary feelings) were probably his *fears* that something had happened to the boy, his *hurt* that his son did not care enough to call to say he would be out so late, and his *frustration* at not knowing how to get in touch with the boy to find out if he was safe. Recognizing and explaining these primary feelings to his son would probably be more productive—have a better effect on the relationship and have more effect on the son's subsequent behavior—than will the actions that are likely to result from the secondary feeling of anger. Exploring the underlying primary feelings will also be more productive for the father in helping him calm down and think of alternative things to say and do when he does confront his son.

Generally, identifying primary feelings is a very productive activity, especially in situations where destructive secondary feelings have arisen or are likely to arise. What we are saying is that although expressing your feelings is crucial to constructive communication, the expression of some feelings is more constructive than the expression of others. Expressing anger, resentment, or jealousy often leads to defensiveness and to arguments. When you are feeling and behaving defensively, you are usually *not* expressing your true feelings and are striking out at the other person instead. Obviously, this is not very constructive. Expressing hurt, pain, frustration, or fear does not lead to defensiveness as often because these feelings aren't usually directed toward hurting someone. We won't be telling you not to express anger, resentment, etc., but we would like you to be aware of their negative effects so you can begin to find alternatives to avoid destructive anger. Anger is usually much harder on you than the person you are angry with. Think about the last time you were angry, and think about the energy it took to deal with it. When you feel anger, we encourage you to work back to the feelings underlying the anger and resentment and express these less destructive feelings. You will often find that once you have expressed these feelings, your anger will go away or not develop at all. That is the major advantage of learning to recognize and express primary feelings.

But before we can express these primary feelings, we must learn to identify them; and since these feelings are often not registered or are overlooked as one progresses through a sequence of feelings, most of us need some instruction before we are able to identify and express them.

GOAL

We want you to be able to recognize when you are expressing secondary feelings (such as anger, resentment, and hostility) because they are indicators that primary feelings (like fear, frustration, emotional hurt, physical pain) have been aroused. Once you learn to identify secondary feelings, you can use this recognition as a trigger or mechanism for beginning an exploration of underlying primary feelings. This exploration will pave the way for a more productive expression of your feelings.

In this chapter, you'll be taking your first step toward the goal of expressing feelings more productively — the identification of primary and secondary feelings.

DEFINITION

Primary Feelings include fear, frustration, emotional hurt, and physical pain. These feelings usually occur most immediately in an emotional situation. They are not usually destructive or coercive and can be readily expressed and dealt with by most people. When you are aware of and can identify your primary feelings, you are better able to act in your own best interest.

Secondary Feelings include anger, resentment, and hostility and are those feelings that may occur immediately after primary feelings. They are often so powerful and coercive that they can conceal primary feelings. These feelings often result in destructive communication and are very difficult for most people to deal with directly. When you are experiencing secondary feelings, very often you will be unable to act in your best interest.

 # ELABORATION

In an emotional situation, an individual is likely to experience a variety of emotional and physical feelings. Often these feelings overlap, and at times are even contradictory. Most of these feelings can be identified as either primary or secondary feelings. They are labeled as such because of the order in which they occur. Primary feelings *precede* secondary feelings, even if only fleetingly. We'll talk about secondary feelings first since they are generally stronger, more prone to produce action, and are most readily recognized.

Secondary Feelings

The most common secondary feelings are anger, hostility, and resentment; however, there are many variations of these feelings, (e.g., irritation, rage, hysteria, despair, and defensiveness). Having experienced these feelings at one time or another, you can recognize how powerful they are. They require an enormous amount of your energy to deal with, and they tend to interfere with your control of your behavior. In addition, they are coercive because they often produce behavior which is used to defend and hurt. An angry or jealous individual very often tries to pressure his or her partner into feeling guilty or inferior by what he or she says or does. When you act on secondary feelings, you are usually *not* in control of your behavior and, therefore, are likely to behave in a manner that you later regret. At the same time, these powerful feelings tend to conceal some of the other important feelings that provide useful information about yourself. These are primary feelings.

Primary Feelings

Primary feelings include emotional feelings of hurt, fear, and frustration, as well as physical feelings of pain, hunger, thirst, sexual arousal, and fatigue. Having experienced these feelings at some time, you are aware that some of them may be uncomfortable and can require massive amounts of your energy to deal with. They can also interfere with your control of your behavior, just as secondary feelings do. But, losing control at the primary level is not usually as destructive to others as it is at the secondary level. For example, if you lose control of your behavior while you are angry, you are very likely to try to hurt someone else. However, if you lose control while feeling sad or hurt, you are less likely to strike out at those you care for or try to make them feel guilty or inferior.

An important point to be made is that any secondary feeling has been preceded by one or more primary feelings, but these primary feelings are often concealed and overpowered by the secondary feelings. So what we say about primary feelings is true only when the individual is aware of their existence and is not experiencing only his or her secondary feelings. It is also important to note that since you are less likely to lash out at your partner when you are aware of your primary feelings, feelings can be much easier for both of you to deal with productively. Defensiveness can be minimized.

Recognizing Potentially Dangerous Secondary Feelings

One of the most important reasons for learning how to work back to primary feelings is that very intense secondary feelings can be extremely destructive and even life-threatening. Extreme anger and rage have been known to result in violence and homicide. Some statistics show that as many as 20 percent of homicides occur between husbands and wives. In most of these cases, one partner has become enraged and lost control of his or her behavior. Many of these individuals would almost certainly have acted differently had they been more in tune with their primary feelings.

Every secondary feeling has an extremely intense form that is potentially very destructive. Jealousy, anger, and resentment can all lead to uncontrollable rage or fury. You can see that it is essential that you deal with your feelings *before* you become so angry or desperate that you can't control your behavior. Identifying and expressing your primary feelings is one of the best ways to do this.

Let's take for example a woman who has just discovered that her partner has been having an affair with another woman for a number of years. She becomes uncontrollably angry, runs out of the house, and drives away. Eventually she calls her partner and tells him that she's going to commit suicide. Even if she doesn't actually kill herself, this woman's actions are terribly destructive both to her partner and to herself. If she has children, she may especially regret the effect it has on them. She is, of course, angry, resentful, and jealous, but primarily she is terribly hurt and afraid. Had she been more aware of these primary feelings, she probably would have chosen a less destructive course of action.

Here's another example. Most child or partner abuse is caused by an individual who has lost control of his or her behavior. For instance, a man who beats up his partner has gone beyond the kind of anger that he can control. For this man, it is absolutely essential that he learn enough about his primary and secondary feelings to recognize the point at which he loses control. It is in his best interest to avoid reaching that point, because once he goes beyond it, he becomes *incapable* of acting in his best interest. He is *not* exercising self-responsibility if he becomes so angry or desperate that he can't control his behavior.

EXAMPLES

FOLLOWING ARE three examples that show how primary feelings precede secondary feelings. For each example, a scenario is presented describing an individual's reaction to a situation. Then the primary feelings experienced are listed. Finally, there is a commentary giving further details.

EXAMPLE 1

Scenario

Kay and her children are spending the day waterskiing. At one point Kay is driving the boat and towing her son, Jeff. Suddenly a powerboat going very fast cuts in front of Jeff and causes him to fall. Kay's immediate reaction is fury and she screams at the driver of the other boat. Kay's extreme anger is an intense secondary feeling. Let's take a look at the other things going on for Kay. The feelings immediately preceding her anger were:

—fear that her son had been hurt.

—frustration at not being able to prevent the near accident.

—frustration at not being able to get to her son any faster to see if he was okay.

—hurt that Jeff was frightened so badly by the other driver's carelessness.

COMMENTARY

Note that all of these primary feelings flashed through Kay's mind so rapidly that she probably failed to register them. This is typical in such a situation.

 EXAMPLE 2

Scenario

Cora and Ben have been together for about 15 years. Most of the time when they have intercourse, Ben ejaculates too soon for Cora. Lately, whenever this happens, Cora becomes very resentful and hostile. These are secondary feelings. It may appear, at first, that Cora had no primary feelings that came before her anger. In Cora's case, this situation has been going on for so many years that she no longer feels the primary feelings. Her feelings go immediately to resentment and hostility. However, years ago she registered some very intense primary feelings. Let's take a look at those feelings. Years ago, when Ben ejaculated too soon for her, Cora felt:

—hurt because she thought he didn't care enough to wait.

—fear that this would always happen and she would always be left unsatisfied.

—fear that there was something physically wrong with him.

—frustrated at not knowing what to do.

—fear that somehow her inadequacy was the cause of the problem.

—hurt for him because he would be upset too.

—frustration due to frequent sexual arousal without being orgasmic.

—pain, occasional pelvic cramping and heaviness due to unrelieved sexual tensions.

COMMENTARY

These primary feelings gradually stopped registering as Cora became hardened to the situation. Then and now, it would be far more constructive for Cora to focus on and express her primary feelings.

EXAMPLE 3

Scenario

Gordon's 13-year-old son has become an avid carpenter, and he frequently borrows Gordon's tools. Most of the time he fails to put them away and, consequently, Gordon can never find them when he wants them. Some of the tools have been lost. Gordon has asked his son repeatedly to put the tools away, pointing out the obvious reasons for doing so. One afternoon, he drives up and his tools are scattered all over the driveway along with one of his son's projects. The boy is nowhere to be seen. Gordon becomes very angry, which is a secondary feeling. Let's take a look at the primary feelings that, at present and over time, preceded the anger. Before getting angry, Gordon felt:

—frustrated because he didn't know how to get his son to pick up after himself.

—hurt that his son didn't seem to care about his wishes or respect his property.

—fear that his son would develop even more thoughtless habits.

COMMENTARY

Gordon would probably find it much more effective to express primary feelings to his son rather than only his anger.

PRACTICE

FOLLOWING IS a practice exercise. Unlike other chapters where you don't have to do all of the practice, in this chapter we'd like you to complete the entire exercise. Be sure to write out your answers. You'll notice that at the end of the exercise you're directed to go through the practice again with several other incidents. It's up to you how many times you practice, but you'll find this type of exercise valuable in helping you get into the habit of identifying your feelings.

Think back to the last time you were angry and work through the incident to identify the sequence of your feelings. We suggest that you record the following:

1. Your immediate reaction.

_____

_____

_____

2. Was the immediate reaction the result of primary or secondary feelings?

_____

_____

_____

3. Work back to the primary feelings that preceded your anger and record these primary feelings.

_____

_____

_____

4. Describe your secondary feelings.

_____

_____

_____

5. Now, write down any primary feelings that may have occurred over time and are no longer registering.

_____

_____

_____

6. If you could relive the experience, how would you handle it differently?

_____

_____

_____

Practice this exercise with several incidents where you have experienced anger or other secondary feelings.

CHAPTER 4

DEALING WITH ANGER

INTRODUCTION

PRIMARY AND secondary feelings each have a range of intensity. Recognizing feelings when they are of low intensity, and dealing with them then, can prevent the problems of having to deal with very high intensity feelings. You've probably realized in going through the previous chapter how many of your feelings involve extremely intense secondary feelings such as anger, resentment, and jealousy. But notice also the other, less intense feelings that exist side-by-side with anger: hurt, irritation, discomfort, excitement, fear. These feelings are less destructive than anger and are often overlooked. In the exercises you've just done, you've had a chance to look at a greater range of the feelings you experience. Being aware of these feelings in a conflict situation can help you deal more constructively with anger. This is of critical importance because anger, if not handled effectively, can prevent you from acting in your best interest. The angrier you become, the harder it is to think beyond the moment, and the more likely you are to do or say something you'll regret later.

GOAL

We want you to be able to deal with anger more constructively. In this chapter, we'll be presenting a strategy that can help you learn to do this. We'd like you to be able to use this strategy when you are angry to better control your own behavior.

1. Learn to identify when you are becoming angry.

2. When you are angry, try to identify and express your primary feelings.

3. Recognize that any feeling has a range of intensity, and it is better to express feelings before they get so intense as to be uncontrollable.

4. When a conflict situation gets out of control, take a break; get away from the situation in order to calm yourself, so more productive communication can occur later.

You may be saying to yourself, "Sure, it's easy to talk about what to do; but when I get angry, it's a lot harder to do." And you're right—it is more difficult to act in your best interest when you are angry. That's why we think you will find it helpful to learn this strategy for dealing with anger. Hopefully, next time you get into a conflict, you'll remember what you learned here and use it to help you deal more constructively with the situation. We'll go over each of the major points in more detail.

1. Learn to identify when you are becoming angry.

This is an extremely critical step. It is considerably easier to exercise self-responsibility when you are aware of your feelings. The sooner you discover feelings of irritation or anger, the sooner you can begin to deal with them effectively. The earliest indication is usually that you feel uncomfortable. Here are some things you might notice about yourself that could serve to warn you that you are getting angry:

- You feel like trying to make your partner feel guilty or inferior.
- You feel like deliberately doing or saying something mean.
- You are beginning to lose sight of what the conflict was about.
- You feel quiet and withdrawn (like the calm before the storm).
- You feel there are fewer and fewer ways to back down gracefully.
- You care more about winning than being right.

- You feel like you need a drink.
- You notice yourself chain-smoking.
- You notice any of the following:
    - Your voice is getting louder.
    - Your fists are clenched.
    - Your face feels flushed.
    - Your heart is beating faster.
    - You feel restless or tense.
    - Your stomach feels knotted.
    - You begin to perspire.

Each person has his or her own warning signals, and you may discover several of your own in the list above. Try to identify others.

2. When you are angry, try to identify and express primary feelings.

You remember from Chapter Three that your primary feelings are those that occur first. There are three simple reasons for trying to express your primary feelings. One is that it will make you feel better to talk about your feelings; not just the anger, but the hurt or fear behind the anger. Another reason is that recognizing and expressing primary feelings can cause your secondary feelings to lessen or to go away altogether. You can save yourself the discomfort of being angry while still expressing your feelings and confronting the issues involved. The third reason is that expressing your primary feelings has a far more constructive impact on your loved ones than expressing anger. They are more likely to be open to what you say and to understand how you feel.

We are not suggesting that you never express your anger when you feel it. It is how you choose to express it that counts. Say you're angry if it will make you feel better. But go beyond that and express your primary feelings as well.

3. Recognize that any feeling has a range of intensity and that it is better to express feelings before they become so intense as to be uncontrollable.

We've talked several times now about how difficult it is to exercise self-responsibility when you are experiencing powerful secondary feelings like anger. As we've said before, the angrier you become, the harder it is to think beyond the moment and the more likely you are to do something you'll regret later. Your alternatives get fewer and less desirable as the situation gets worse.

In most conflict situations, the feelings early on are of relatively low intensity. At low intensity, annoyance, impatience, and frustration feel uncomfortable, but they are not destructive. Anger and rage, on the other hand, are very intense feelings. They feel very uncomfortable to the person experiencing them and can be extremely destructive to all involved. Certainly venting anger and resentment may make you feel better for the moment, but if you've created a situation that you later regret, you have not acted in your best interest.

Keeping yourself aware of the scope and intensity of your feelings will help you notice the warning signals that tell you you're losing control. There is no single point at which you should stop yourself, it's a matter of degree, but the earlier the better. The sooner you can register and identify an uncomfortable feeling, the less effort it takes to remedy the situation. What you want to avoid is reaching the extreme and doing or saying something you'll really regret later. Again, this is something only you can know about yourself. Sometimes you may allow yourself to say hurtful things you know you don't mean just to vent your anger. You may feel that your relationship is strong enough to handle this. At the other extreme, physical violence is something no relationship can adjust to constructively. Once you've hit someone you care about, you have done something you cannot undo later. Anger can scar and disfigure relationships emotionally and physically when it is vented irresponsibly.

We recognize that most of you have probably been conditioned not to express feelings of minor annoyance or frustration. You've probably been taught not to make a big deal over "little things." "Wait till it becomes a real issue," you've been told. The problem with this is if you wait until your annoyance gets so out of hand that you can't ignore it any longer, you've missed out on a lot of calmer, more pleasant solutions to the problem. Now you have to deal with the situation while angry and least able to act in your best interest. This conditioning will be hard to overcome but you can see how important it is to try.

4. When a conflict situation gets out of control, take a break.

One of the most destructive things that can happen in a conflict situation is that you will argue the problem to a point of no return. Many people think that once they get into a conflict, they should stick with it till they iron it out. There are times when this strategy works well, but when one or both individuals are angry and out of control, this approach can be terribly destructive. Nothing can be resolved in such a situation. It is far more constructive to learn how to be comfortable leaving loose ends for a while. You can come back to the problem later and start over when you feel calmer.

How do you know when you are out of control? It's actually pretty obvious if you stop long enough to observe your behavior. That's why *staying* aware of your feelings is so important. Once you are aware that you are either losing control or are out of control already, you need to stop and take your leave.

This is hard to do because it is difficult to express yourself constructively when you are angry. Try practicing what you will say next time you need to get out of a situation, and then use that line when you need it. Discuss with your partner some signals to help him or her recognize that you are saying you need to stop for now.

EXAMPLES

FOLLOWING ARE three examples that show what happens when feelings become very intense and anger is not dealt with constructively. For each example, a scenario is presented describing an individual progressing from low to high intensity feelings and losing control. The commentary explains how each situation could have been improved had the individual used the strategy presented in this chapter.

EXAMPLE 1

Scenario

Phoebe has just spent a busy day cleaning house in preparation for a party she and Roy are having. Roy has been home all day doing some chores around the house. Phoebe feels irritated that, even though he's doing things that need to be done, he had to pick today to do them. She wishes he would offer to help her or watch the children. She let this feeling go, though, thinking it too insignificant to bring up. However, the irritation persists. At one point, she comments sarcastically about Roy's choice of chores. He detects that Phoebe is annoyed and questions her about it. She makes a lot of accusations. He becomes defensive, and before long they are having a heated argument. Things get worse and worse until Phoebe's feelings become so intense that she throws her Swedish meatballs into the sink, tells Roy to call off the party, and locks herself in her room.

COMMENTARY

This situation may not have turned out so destructively had Phoebe been better able to deal with her anger. Her irritation at Roy's choice of chores was the first indication that she was becoming angry. At that point she could have averted her anger by expressing her irritation and the other primary feelings she was experiencing at the time (i.e., frustration over too much work and too little time; hurt that Roy didn't notice this and offer to help).

 # EXAMPLE 2

Scenario

Lew and Joan are at a party one night with some friends from college. Lew notices that Joan is talking with her former fiance. He watches for a while and becomes alarmed that they seem to be enjoying themselves so much. He's convinced that other people at the party have noticed, too. He feels jealous and resentful that Joan would put him in such an awkward position. Not wanting to make a scene, he says nothing but goes into the other room for a drink. For the next hour he stays away from her and drinks heavily. When he finally returns, he sees that Joan and her ex-fiance are still talking intensely. Lew approaches Joan and announces that he might as well go home since he isn't having any fun and that she can do whatever she pleases. She becomes concerned and follows him outside, where they get into an argument about whether she was flirting or not. The dispute goes on loudly for over 30 minutes and results in neighbors calling the police about the noise.

COMMENTARY

Lew could have dealt with his anger more constructively had he used the strategy presented in this chapter. First of all, he tried to ignore the early indications that he was becoming angry. He might have been able to avert his anger by calling Joan away for a moment to let her know how he was feeling. While he was still calm and sober, his primary feelings were probably a mixture of hurt and fear. Dealing with those feelings at that point would probably have prevented them from becoming so intense. Even later, during the argument outside, Lew or Joan could have averted trouble with the police had they realized they were both out of control. The best time to stop and take a break is as early as possible in the argument.

EXAMPLE 3

Scenario

Rita and Cliff have been together for about five years. Cliff is 15 years older than Rita. She is in her late twenties now and is becoming bored with their sex life. She hasn't discussed her boredom and dissatisfaction with Cliff, and she is a little resentful that he hasn't noticed. She knows that she loves Cliff and she tries a number of things to enhance their sexual encounters. Finally, she gets up enough courage to show him a book demonstrating a variety of sexual positions. She suggests they try some of them. He laughs at the book and tells her she's got too much imagination for her own good. She gets furious and tells him that since he's so sexually uninteresting, somebody's got to make up for his lack of imagination. She adds that if he finds that whole subject so funny, he can just do without sex. As a final insult, she says that he is so boring he might as well be impotent.

COMMENTARY

Rita could have avoided her explosive reaction at the end of the scenario had she dealt with her anger more constructively. Her first warnings that she was becoming angry were her feelings of boredom, dissatisfaction, and resentment. Had she expressed these and her primary feelings to Cliff, the situation would probably have turned out quite differently. Rita's resentment could have been handled more constructively by both of them and wouldn't have turned into such destructive hostility.

PRACTICE

FOLLOWING ARE several practice exercises. As in the previous chapter, we'd like you to do all of them. Be sure to write out your answers. Exercises 2 through 4 can be especially valuable to you if you spend some time thinking about your responses and are as thorough as possible. Hopefully, the next time you're in a conflict situation, you will remember and use what you've written here.

1. Write down, in your own words, the four major points of the strategy for dealing with anger.

   1. _____

   2. _____

   3. _____

   4. _____

2. Go over the list of common indicators for becoming angry, and write down the ones that apply to you. Then think carefully and add any other personal indicators that tell you you're becoming angry.

   _____

   _____

   _____

   _____

   _____

   _____

   _____

   _____

   _____

   _____

3. Think about the last time you were so angry you lost control and said or did something you really regretted. Write down the warnings that could have helped you to stop earlier and take a break.

_____

_____

_____

_____

_____

_____

_____

_____

_____

_____

_____

4. Write down three things you could say next time you feel you want to discontinue an argument. Think of things that make your feelings and condition clear and that you would feel comfortable saying. For example, you could say, "I'm feeling too upset to go on right now. I'd like to stop for a while."

1. _____

2. _____

3. _____

CHAPTER 5

USING "I" LANGUAGE

INTRODUCTION

FOR PEOPLE who love and care for each other, "I" language is a most effective way of communicating because when it is being used, it is impossible to argue. Three of the most common mistakes that lead to arguing are:

- Statements about the way another person feels.
- Questions that mask intentions and for which there is no comfortable answer.
- Questions that ask for justification of feelings or behavior.

Any of the above statements or questions can lead to defensiveness and the urge to retaliate — prime ingredients for an argument. "I" language can prevent arguments because it discourages the use of the above types of statements and questions. When you and your partner both use "I" language:

- You will be able to talk about your *own* feelings, desires, and perceptions. You will be accepted as the world's authority on yourself; therefore, your feelings and perceptions about yourself will not be argued.
- You will be able to state your feelings, desires, concerns, intentions, and opinions openly rather than hiding them behind questions.
- Feelings will be accepted as fact and you won't be asked to justify the way you feel.

No doubt you're wondering how "I" language can accomplish what we say it can. One way is by changing the way you use language to express yourself. That's what you'll be learning in this chapter. But "I" language is more than a language or a way of expressing yourself.

It is an attitude as well and without the attitude, it is less likely that just using the language will help you communicate more effectively. In other words, it's the attitude coupled with the language that makes "I" language most effective. Following is an explanation of the four principles that describe the attitude we're talking about.

1. **Say what is true for you.** In other words, be honest about your feelings. Sometimes you won't know how you feel, but say what you do know and be truthful. Obviously, communication can't be very effective when you don't represent your feelings accurately.

2. **Believe what you hear.** Believing what you hear is a matter of trusting your partner to say what is true for him or her. At times this is difficult for some people. For instance, suppose a woman tells her partner that she loves him. They've been having some arguments lately and he isn't sure he believes her. Where does this leave them? She's feeling hurt that he doesn't believe her, and she feels pressured to try and prove her love. He's feeling insecure. About all they can talk about is whether she really loves him or not. Until he believes that what she says is true for her, effective communication will be difficult, if not impossible. Believing what your partner says does represent a risk sometimes, but it is well worth it because it makes interpersonal communication so much more constructive.

3. **Believe that you're both on the same side.** Here again we are talking about trust. Many couples wind up having difficulty communicating because they see themselves as being on opposite sides. When two people love each other, it is assumed that they want the best for each other and that they won't deliberately try to hurt one another. When you trust that your partner will be considerate of your feelings and that he or she will not try to hurt you, you can feel far more comfortable being open and honest about your feelings and desires. Since openness and honesty are critical in personal communication, trusting that you're on the same side is essential.

4. **Accept your partner.** This doesn't mean you have to like everything your partner says or does. For example, you may dislike it when your partner smokes, but judging this behavior or refusing to accept it will probably not change it — and certainly not without creating resentment in both parties. There will be many things about your partner that he or she will not change. And for the most part, you will find yourself a lot happier accepting these things as realities.

We'd like to point out that you can change only your own communication behavior. You cannot directly modify your partner's behavior if he or she doesn't

88

want to change. Don't be discouraged by this. You will find that your communications will improve significantly even if only you are using "I" language. Also, if your partner is resisting using "I" language, setting a good example yourself will improve your chances of persuading him or her of the value of "I" language.

GOAL

We want you to be able to converse with the people you love or care for in "I" language. In this chapter, you will be taking your first steps toward this goal. You will be asked to identify when "I" language is and is not being used. You'll also be asked to translate into "I" language phrases and sentences that are not "I" language.

DEFINITION

"I" language is a verbal way of expressing information about your own desires, goals, and feelings. "I" language is also an attitude.

The rules for using "I" language are:

1. Start every sentence about feelings with the pronoun "I" rather than with second or third person pronouns.

2. Use verbs that imply "want" rather than "should."

3. Make your feelings or concerns known *before* asking a question rather than hiding them behind a question.

4. When inquiring about another person's feelings or behavior, limit yourself to asking *what* the person is feeling rather than asking for justification of those feelings.

5. Stick to how you or another person is feeling or behaving now rather than generalizing about the past or predicting the future.

6. Be conscientious in expressing what you know about your feelings and desires. When you don't know, commit yourself to finding out and letting the other person know rather than just saying, "I don't know," "I don't care."

NOTE:

Be aware that when you first start using "I" language, it may feel awkward or stilted. We would like to assure you that the more you practice using "I" language, the more natural it will sound to you.

⬥⬥ ELABORATION ⬥⬥

Using "I" language can greatly enhance communication between two people who care for each other. In "I" language you express only your own desires, goals, and feelings. If you are expressing the feelings of another person or if you are expressing feelings you think you should have, but don't, then you're not using "I" language.

Use of "I" language is ensured when these rules are followed:

1. Start every sentence about feelings with the pronoun "I."

Avoid starting sentences with "you," "we," "let's," "that's," "I think you," or "you said."

Examples

I'm unhappy.

I feel rejected.

I'd like to go to the show.

I don't feel that way.

Note that the use of "I" indicates the person is speaking of his own feelings and taking responsibility for making those feelings known.

Nonexamples

You're making me unhappy.

I feel you're rejecting me.

Let's go to the show.

You're wrong about that.

The pronouns above indicate that the speaker is not taking responsibility for making his feelings known and, in the first two statements, is actually blaming someone else for his feelings.

2. Use verbs that imply "want."

Avoid using verbs that imply "should," "ought," or "have to."

Examples

I'd like to get the laundry done.

I want to take the kids to the zoo.

I feel like getting everything fixed around the house.

Note that the verbs used above indicate that the speaker is exercising self-responsibility by acknowledging his desires.

Nonexamples

I ought to get the laundry done.

I should take the kids to the zoo.

I have to get everything fixed around the house.

The verbs used above all indicate that the speaker is allowing his actions to be influenced by something other than his own desires.

Think about this: if you can't replace a "should" with a "want," you're probably not exercising self-responsibility. You may be doing something you don't want to do for someone else or out of some sense of duty. Reconsider whether it is in *your* best interest.

3. Make your feelings or concerns known *before* asking a question.

Don't hide your concerns, opinions, feelings, or desires behind a question.

Examples

I'm worried about your silence. I'd like to know if something is bothering you.

I get really discouraged about things being in such a mess and I'd like your help in resolving this.

I hear you saying you're not upset, but I also hear you yelling.

I'm hungry and I was wondering if you were hungry too.

Note that in the above examples the speaker makes his concerns and opinions clear before or instead of asking a question. This allows a person to answer more freely without feeling trapped.

Nonexamples

Why are you so quiet?

Why don't you ever pick up after yourself?

Do you always yell when you're not upset?

Aren't you hungry yet?

The examples above make it very difficult for a person to answer without feeling trapped and defensive. All of the questions above imply that the speaker really has something else on his mind. In the first and last questions, the speaker is already thinking of an answer and in the other two, questions are used to hide sarcastic opinions.

4. When inquiring about another person's feelings or behavior, limit yourself to asking *what* that person is feeling.

Don't ask others to justify why they feel the way they do or why they behave the way they do.

Examples

I feel a little uncomfortable because you seem tense to me this evening. I'd like to know if something is upsetting you.

I wish you hadn't had such a hard day. Is there anything I can do to help make it better?

I feel perfectly comfortable when things are disheveled. I'd like to know how you feel.

Note that in the examples above the speaker limits himself to finding out what the feelings are and what can be done. There are no assumptions made and no requests for justification. The person can answer without having to defend, deny, or justify himself.

Nonexamples

Why are you so tense and upset?

Why do you let yourself get so upset over one lousy day?

Why are you so picky?

The examples above would most likely result in defensive behavior because the person feels he has to justify something that may not make any sense to someone else. "Why" is irrelevant because feelings are facts. Questioning why they exist can lead to depression as a result of endless self-analysis. Since you are the world's authority on yourself, you either know or you don't.

5. Stick to how you or another person is feeling or behaving now. Use phrases like "up until now" or "in the past."

Don't generalize about the past or predict future feelings or behavior. Avoid using words like "always" and "never."

Examples

I'm unhappy at the way this has been handled in the past and I'm afraid it can't be solved.

I'm afraid you'll think I'm silly for feeling this way. I'd like to know how you really feel.

In the past I haven't been able to get through to you. I hope I can make myself clear this time.

Note that in the examples above the speaker is concentrating on present feelings or checking out past feelings. The speaker is not assuming that what has occurred in the past will occur again. This is critical because people's feelings and behavior change.

Nonexamples

I'm unhappy at the way this problem has been handled in the past. You'll never change, will you?

You probably think I'm acting silly like you always do.

You never listen to me and you never will.

In the examples above, the speaker is predicting how the other person will feel or behave based on past experience. The speaker is assuming that the other person's feelings and behavior will never change.

6. Be conscientious in expressing what you know about your feelings and desires. When you don't know, commit yourself to finding out and letting the other person know.

Don't say, "I don't know," or "I don't care," when you do know and you do care. When you honestly don't know, don't just leave it at that.

Examples

I know how I feel about this, but it's going to take some time and energy to explain.

I don't know what I think about that, but I'll work on it and let you know when I figure it out.

I don't have much depth of feeling about what we eat tonight except that I'm not in the mood for anything rich. I'm open to suggestions.

Note that in the statements above the speaker is giving whatever information he knows about his feelings or preferences.

Nonexamples

Oh, I just don't know.

I don't know.

I don't care what we eat.

In the statements above, the speaker is being lazy about expressing his feelings and preferences. In the second example, he says, "I don't know," and leaves the listener hanging.

92

The following is a summary of the information detailed in the preceding elaboration. You may find it helpful when studying the conversations in the sample conversation and practice sections.

"I" Language	NOT "I" Language
1. Sentences about feelings that begin with: **I**	1. Sentences about feelings that begin with: **You, We, I think you, Let's, You said, That's, etc.**
2. Verbs implying want or desire such as: **Want, Prefer, Like, Feel**	2. Verbs implying "should" such as: **Should, Must, Ought, Need to, Have to, Supposed to, Got to, etc.**
3. Statements making the speaker's concerns and feelings clear *before* asking a question.	3. Questions that imply that: **The speaker has something on his mind. The speaker wants a particular answer. No matter what the answer, the speaker will be critical. The speaker is actually expressing an opinion sarcastically.**
4. Questions that: **Ask what the person feels. Ask what a person wants to do. Ask what can be done to help. Etc.**	4. Questions that: **Ask why a person feels the way they do. Ask why a person behaves the way they do.**
5. Statements or questions that: **Deal with what a person feels now. Check out whether a person's past feelings are still accurate.**	5. Words and phrases that indicate generalizing or predicting such as: **Always, Probably, Never, (You) will, Won't/Don't ever, (You) are, All the time, Going to, etc.**
6. Statements that indicate that the speaker is being conscientious in expressing what he knows about his feelings such as: **I don't know, but I'll let you know when I do. I don't have much depth of feeling on the subject, but I prefer...**	6. Phrases that indicate that the speaker is not being conscientious about expressing what he knows about his feelings such as: **I don't know. I don't care. Anything you want.**

SAMPLE CONVERSATIONS

FOLLOWING ARE five sets of sample conversations. The first conversation in each set presents a couple communicating *without* using "I" language. In the commentary next to each of these conversations remarks are made about each statement. Read these commentaries only if you need help understanding why a statement is or is not "I" language.

The second conversation in each set presents a similar conversation in which the couple *is* using "I" language. You will notice that the overall tone and outcome of the "I" language conversations are very different.

Read through only as many samples as you need to be able to recognize and correct instances where "I" language is not being used.

Below is a sample conversation in which neither individual is using "I" language consistently. The nonuse of "I" language is indicated by bold italics.

COMMENTARY

Woman: *What would you like to do tonight?*

She is asking a question without making her intentions clear — that she wants to do something with her partner that she likes.

Man: There's a super football game between UCLA and Houston on TV tonight; I'd like to watch it.

Using "I," he expresses what he wants to do.

Woman: *All you ever want* to do is watch football.

She uses "you" to tell him about his behavior. She also generalizes about all he ever wants to do.

Man: What do you mean? I only watched twice this week.

He reacts defensively.

Woman: Well, somehow I *never* get to do what I want to do.

Using "never," she generalizes about the situation.

Man: What would you like to do?

He asks her what she'd like to do, which is acceptable since he's already made his preference clear.

Woman: Oh, *I don't know;* anything but watch football.

By saying, "I don't know," she is **not** being conscientious about expressing her feelings. Chances are she **does** know what she wants and if she doesn't, she can tell him that she'll think about it and let him know.

 **"I" Language**

The sample conversation below is similar to the one on the facing page, except that below the individuals are using "I" language consistently. Notice how the overall tone and the outcome differ.

Woman: I'd like to go to the movie with you this evening and I'm wondering what you feel like doing.

Man: There's a super football game between UCLA and Houston on TV tonight; I'd like to watch it.

Woman: I don't really want to watch football, and I would love to have your undivided attention tonight.

Man: I feel strongly about seeing this particular game, but it's over at nine and I'd enjoy doing something with you then. Would you be too tired to go to a late show?

Sample Conversation 2

Below is a sample conversation in which neither individual is using "I" language consistently. The nonuse of "I" language is indicated by bold italics.

COMMENTARY

Man: *Wouldn't you like to go to bed honey?* It's getting late.

He asks a question without making his desires clear — that he's interested in sex.

Woman: I *need* to finish up my homework. *You go ahead if you're so tired.*

She indicates by the use of "need" that she is doing her homework out of a sense of duty rather than desire.

Man: I didn't say I was tired.

He gets annoyed because she's not getting his message.

Woman: Well, *what did you mean when you suggested we go to bed?*

She uses a "you" sentence rather than saying, "I don't know what you mean...."

Man: I thought you might be interested in sex, but then *you never are.*

Using the pronoun "you" he tells her about her behavior and generalizes that she's **never** interested in sex.

Woman: I am too, but I didn't realize that was what you had in mind. *You always expect* me to read your mind.

She generalizes about his behavior: "You **always** expect..."

Man: I sure don't know why I'd expect that since you're so lousy at it.

He talks about her behavior using "you."

Woman: *You probably think* I'm lousy in bed too.

She predicts what he is thinking.

Man: I can't remember if you are or not.

Sarcasm results to cover hurt feelings.

98

The sample conversation below is similar to the one on the facing page, except that below the individuals are using "I" language consistently. Notice how the overall tone and the outcome differ.

Man: I'd like to get into bed with you and make love. What are your feelings about that?

Woman: I'd like to get the rest of my homework out of the way first, but then I'd love to take you up on your idea.

Man: Great! See you in the bedroom.

Below is a sample conversation in which neither individual is using "I" language consistently.

COMMENTARY

Man: *What's wrong with you?*

In essence, he is saying, "Why are you upset?" And he has asked a question without making his concerns clear — he may be worried about her or find her **apparent** depression upsetting to his mood.

Woman: What do you mean, "What's wrong?"

She gets defensive.

Man: Well, *you're* obviously upset about something.

He talks about her feelings using "you."

Woman: No, I'm not upset.

She uses good "I" language.

Man: Sure, *you must be. You've* got that look on your face.

Again, he is talking about her feelings and behavior and using "you."

Woman: What look?

She's confused by his interpretation of her facial expression.

Man: The look that *always* means, "look out!"

He generalizes about what her facial expression **always** means.

Woman: *You're* imagining things. There's nothing wrong.

She talks about his behavior and uses "you."

Man: Oh, come on! *Why are you denying it?*

Here, he asks her why she acts the way she does.

Woman: I'm NOT upset!

She is getting upset and frustrated because he won't believe her.

Man: *Then why are you yelling?*

He asks a question that barely conceals his satisfaction at having been right all along.

100

The sample conversation below is similar to the one on the facing page, except that below the individuals are using "I" language consistently. Notice how the overall tone and the outcome differ.

Man: I'm concerned about you. I'm wondering if anything is bothering you.

Woman: No, there's nothing bothering me.

Man: I wondered because your face looked troubled.

Woman: I've just been trying to remember where I put an important receipt.

Man: Is it something I can help with?

Woman: No, and it's really not that important.

Below is a sample conversation in which neither individual is using "I" language consistently.

COMMENTARY

Man: I really *should* get the yard work done this weekend.

Using "should," he indicates that he is acting out of a sense of obligation rather than desire.

Woman: I was hoping you'd take me shopping. *We* really *ought* to get the wallpaper for the bathroom before my folks come.

She uses "we" and indicates that both of them "ought to" shop for wallpaper rather than talking about her own **desire** to do it.

Man: What do you mean "we"? *I've got to* get all this stuff done and you want me to shop for wallpaper?

He objects to the use of "we" and then goes on to talk about what he **has** to do.

Woman: Well, *we ought* to make the decision together. I guess *you don't care* if the bathroom looks like a mess when my folks come.

Again, she uses "we" and talks about what they both "ought to" do.

Man: *Do you really think they'll care so much that it'll ruin their visit?* Besides, you *never* agree with me on decorating decisions anyway.

He asks a question that conceals his opinion — that her folks won't really miss the wallpaper. He also generalizes about her behavior using "never."

Woman: *Why are you being so argumentative?*

She asks him why he is behaving the way he is.

"I" Language

The sample conversation below is similar to the one on the facing page, except that below the individuals are using "I" language consistently. Notice how the overall tone and the outcome differ.

Man: I want to get the yard work done over the weekend.

Woman: I was hoping you'd take me shopping. I'd like to get wallpaper for the bathroom before my folks come. Would you have any time to help me out?

Man: I'm interested, but at this point I don't think I'll have any time. What did you want to do?

Woman: Well, I like sharing decorating decisions with you, and I don't want to get something you don't like.

Man: If you narrow the choice down to two or three samples and bring them home, it would save me time and I'll be happy to give you my input. Or, call me from the shop after you've looked around and I'll run over for a few minutes.

Sample Conversation 5

Below is a sample conversation in which neither individual is using "I" language consistently.

COMMENTARY

Man: I'm getting my Christmas list together. What would you like this year?

He uses "I" language to announce his intentions before asking a question.

Woman: *I don't know.* Surprise me.

By saying, "I don't know," she is **not** being conscientious about expressing her desires. She probably has some ideas about what she wants. If not, she can tell him that she'll give it some thought and let him know.

Man: I don't feel comfortable about doing that.

He uses "I" language to express his feelings.

Woman: Well, *I don't care* what you get me as long as you pick it.

By saying, "I don't care," she is **not** being conscientious about expressing her feelings. She **does** care what he gives her.

Man: I do that *every* year and *you never like* what I choose.

He talks about her behavior using "you" and generalizes that she **never** likes what he gives her.

Woman: I didn't like the hunting rifle you got me last year. *How stupid can you get? You just did that to be mean.*

She uses "you" to put down his behavior and his motives.

Man: I'd hoped you would get involved and start hunting with me.

He uses "I" language to express his wants.

Woman: I bet! *You just wanted* another gun for your collection.

Again, she talks about his behavior.

Man: *Why don't you just tell me what you want?* That way I won't get you something you hate.

He asks a question but is really trying to express the opinion that he wants her to tell him what she wants. At the same time, he is asking her why she behaves the way she does.

Woman: *Why don't you know what I'd like?*

She then asks him why **he** behaves the way **he** does.

104

"I" Language

The sample conversation below is similar to the one on the facing page, except that below the individuals are using "I" language consistently. Notice how the overall tone and the outcome differ.

Man: I'm getting my Christmas list together. What would you like this year?

Woman: I'd like to be surprised.

Man: I don't feel comfortable about doing that.

Woman: Well, I don't know right now what I want, but I'll think about it and give you a list.

Man: I feel much better about that.

PRACTICE

FOLLOWING ARE five practice items. Each presents a sample conversation like the ones you looked at in the previous section. In Part A for each item, you are to underline or highlight the phrases, words, or sentences that are *not* "I" language. In Part B, take each instance that you indicated and rewrite it in "I" language. *Don't* recreate the conversation as we did in the sample conversation section. Here we only want you to practice translating specific words, phrases, or sentences into "I" language.

For each part of each item there is feedback on the following pages. The feedback for Part A will show you what words, phrases, and sentences we identified as *not* being "I" language. Don't worry if your underlining or highlighting isn't exactly like ours. As in the sample conversations, the commentary presents remarks about each statement. Read the commentary only if you need help understanding the feedback. Wherever you have questions, use the definition to help you resolve them. In Part B feedback, we have rewritten, in "I" language, those instances we indicated in Part A feedback. Your rewrites probably won't be quite the same in all cases; but again, where you have doubts, check the definition or the list following the elaboration.

After completing each item (both parts) look at the feedback. If you feel you're doing well after the first couple of items, go on to the next chapter. If you seem to be having trouble at any point, go back and look over the definition, elaboration, and sample conversations. When you feel you have resolved the difficulty, continue with the practice.

Part A.

Underline or highlight wherever "I" language is *not* used.

1. **Woman:** Why are you such a slob?

2. **Man:** What!?

3. **Woman:** You never put your clothes in the hamper.

4. **Man:** I wouldn't say never. You're too picky anyway.

5. **Woman:** I am not. We should keep our home neat and clean and that's impossible when you're so sloppy.

6. **Man:** Why can't you just be happy with a slightly less than spotless house?

7. **Woman:** Why can't you do a little thing like put your clothes in the hamper?

8. **Man:** Why do you get so upset over such a little thing?

9. **Woman:** I guess it just seems like a little thing because you have such a little mind.

REMINDER

Don't forget to write your answers.

Part B.

For each phrase or sentence you indicated on the opposite page, rewrite that specific phrase or sentence in "I" language. Remember, the phrases you rewrite won't necessarily make a complete conversation.

1. Woman: _____
   _____

2. Man: _____
   _____

3. Woman: _____
   _____

4. Man: _____
   _____

5. Woman: _____
   _____

6. Man: _____
   _____

7. Woman: _____
   _____

8. Man: _____
   _____

9. Woman: _____
   _____

Part A.

Below, we have indicated instances we identified as not being "I" language. Don't be concerned if your responses are slightly different.

COMMENTARY

1. **Woman:** *Why are you such a slob?*

   She is asking him why he behaves the way he does and at the same time is actually expressing her opinion that he is a slob. Probably what she really feels is that his sloppiness causes her a problem.

2. **Man:** What!?

   He's confused and caught off guard by her question.

3. **Woman:** *You never* put your clothes in the hamper.

   She uses "you" and generalizes about his behavior by saying "never."

4. **Man:** I wouldn't say never. *You're too picky* anyway.

   Using "you," he talks about her behavior.

5. **Woman:** I am not. *We should* keep our home neat and clean and *that's* impossible when *you're* so sloppy.

   "We should" implies that she, at least, is acting out of obligation and including him. "That's" and "you" are also used.

6. **Man:** *Why can't you just be happy with a slightly less than spotless house?*

   He's questioning why and also expressing an opinion.

7. **Woman:** *Why can't you do a little thing like put your clothes in the hamper?*

   She's questioning why and also expressing an opinion.

8. **Man:** *Why do you get so upset over such a little thing?*

   Again, he's questioning why and expressing an opinion.

9. **Woman:** I guess it just seems like a little thing because *you* have such a little mind.

   She uses "you" to talk about his behavior.

110

Part B.

Below, we have rewritten the phrases and sentences indicated on the previous page in "I" language. Your answers may differ so if you're in doubt, check them against the definition to ensure that you have used "I" language.

1. **Woman:** I get very upset when the house is a mess and I'd like to have some help keeping it neat.

2. **Man:**

3. **Woman:** I find your clothes on the floor and around the hamper a lot of the time and I get tired of picking them up to make the room look neat.

4. **Man:** I like to drop them where I please.

5. **Woman:** I like to keep our home neat and clean. I'd really like to have some help in keeping it that way.

6. **Man:** I can be happy with a slightly less than spotless house.

7. **Woman:** I would really appreciate having the clothes put in the hamper because it makes a great difference to me in how the room looks and it saves me work.

8. **Man:** I can see that it's important to you, even though I don't understand why.

9. **Woman:** (This judgmental statement cannot be written in "I" language and is better left unsaid.)

Part A.

Underline or highlight wherever "I" language is *not* used.

1. **Woman:** What would you like for dinner tonight?

2. **Man:** I don't care — it's up to you.

3. **Woman:** Let's have fish sticks.

4. **Man:** We have fish sticks all the time.

5. **Woman:** It's your fault for keeping me on such a tight budget. Fish sticks are cheap.

6. **Man:** Well I'm sick of them! Why can't you serve something else?

7. **Woman:** Like what?

8. **Man:** I don't care — anything but fish sticks.

Part B.

For each phrase or sentence you indicated on the opposite page, rewrite that specific phrase or sentence in "I" language. Remember, the phrases you rewrite won't necessarily make a complete conversation.

1. **Woman:** _____

_____

2. **Man:** _____

_____

3. **Woman:** _____

_____

4. **Man:** _____

_____

5. **Woman:** _____

_____

6. **Man:** _____

_____

7. **Woman:** _____

_____

8. **Man:** _____

_____

FEEDBACK 2

Part A.

Below, we have indicated instances we identified as not being "I" language. Don't be concerned if your responses are slightly different.

COMMENTARY

1. **Woman:** *What would you like for dinner tonight?*

   She has asked a question without making her intentions or preferences clear.

2. **Man:** *I don't care — it's up to you.*

   He is **not** being conscientious about expressing his feelings because he **does** care.

3. **Woman:** *Let's* have fish sticks.

   She includes him by saying "let's."

4. **Man:** *We* have fish sticks *all the time.*

   He generalizes about her behavior, using "all the time." He also uses "we."

5. **Woman:** *It's your fault* for keeping me on such a tight budget. Fish sticks are cheap.

   She blames him, using a variation of "you."

6. **Man:** Well I'm sick of them! *Why can't you serve something else?*

   He asks why she behaves the way she does.

7. **Woman:** *Like what?*

   She still hasn't made her preferences clear.

8. **Man:** *I don't care* — anything but fish sticks.

   Again he says "I don't care" when he actually does care.

Part B.

Below, we have rewritten the phrases and sentences indicated on the previous page in "I" language. Your answers may differ so if you're in doubt, check them against the definition to ensure that you have used "I" language.

1. **Woman:** I'm getting ready to serve dinner and was wondering if you had any preferences.

2. **Man:** I hadn't thought about it much. Nothing special comes to mind, but I'm open to suggestions.

3. **Woman:** I prefer fish sticks.

4. **Man:** I'm feeling a little tired of fish sticks myself.

5. **Woman:** I agree, but I try to stick to our budget and they're cheap.

6. **Man:** I'd like to make an exception and have something else.

7. **Woman:** I'd like fried chicken. What did you have in mind?

8. **Man:** I'm still having trouble thinking of something and I'd like a few more suggestions.

Part A.

Underline or highlight wherever "I" language is *not* used.

1. **Woman:** We sure have a lousy night life!

2. **Man:** What's wrong with our night life?

3. **Woman:** I feel neglected because you're always watching sports on TV.

4. **Man:** Maybe it'd be more interesting if we had sex more often.

5. **Woman:** I'd like that, but I don't feel satisfied lately.

6. **Man:** Is there something you want that you're not getting?

7. **Woman:** Time. I don't have enough time to come before you do.

8. **Man:** I didn't know that. I've been thinking you had an orgasm every time.

9. **Woman:** I faked it sometimes.

10. **Man:** I'm feeling really upset about this and I'd like to talk about it some more to find out what we can do to make it more satisfying for both of us.

Part B.

For each phrase or sentence you indicated on the opposite page, rewrite that phrase or sentence in "I" language.

1. Woman: _____

2. Man: _____

3. Woman: _____

4. Man: _____

5. Woman: _____

6. Man: _____

7. Woman: _____

8. Man: _____

9. Woman: _____

10. Man: _____

Part A.

Below, we have indicated instances we identified as not being "I" language. Don't be concerned if your responses are slightly different.

COMMENTARY

1. **Woman:** ***We sure have a lousy night life!***

She includes him in their lousy night life by using "we."

2. **Man:** What's wrong with our night life?

His question is acceptable here because his intentions are obvious. Her statement has opened the door for him to ask what she means.

3. **Woman:** I feel neglected because ***you're always*** watching sports on TV.

She generalizes about his behavior and uses the pronoun "you."

4. **Man:** Maybe ***it'd*** be more interesting if ***we*** had sex more often.

Using "it'd" and "we," he talks about her wants instead of his own.

5. **Woman:** I'd like that, but I don't feel satisfied lately.

She uses "I" language to talk about her wants and feelings.

6. **Man:** Is there something you want that you're not getting?

His question is acceptable because she has already implied that there is something missing.

7. **Woman:** Time. I don't have enough time to come before you do.

She's still using "I" language.

8. **Man:** I didn't know that. I've been thinking you had an orgasm every time.

He's still using "I" language.

9. **Woman:** I faked it sometimes.

"I" language.

10. **Man:** I'm feeling really upset about this and I'd like to talk about it some more to find out what ***we*** can do to make it more satisfying for both of us.

"I" language except for his use of "we."

Part B.

Below, we have rewritten the phrases and sentences indicated on the previous page in "I" language. Your answers may differ so if you're in doubt, check them against the definition to ensure that you have used "I" language.

1. **Woman:** I'm not happy with our night life.

2. **Man:**

3. **Woman:** I feel neglected when you're watching sports on TV.

4. **Man:** I'd like to have sex more often.

5. **Woman:**

6. **Man:**

7. **Woman:**

8. **Man:**

9. **Woman:**

10. **Man:** I'm feeling upset about this and I'd like to talk about it some more to find out what *I* can do to make it more satisfying for both of us.

PRACTICE 4

Part A.

Underline or highlight wherever "I" language is *not* used.

1. **Man:** What would you like to do on our vacation?

2. **Woman:** I don't know. What would you like to do?

3. **Man:** I'd like to be perfectly frank about what I want and I'd like to hear what you honestly want instead of fooling around with "I don't know — what do you want."

4. **Woman:** Okay, I'd like to go somewhere tropical where I can lie in the sun and watch people.

5. **Man:** I'm not interested in lying in the sun, but I would like to play some sports like volleyball, racquetball, tennis, et cetera. That could be tropica' What kind of night life appeals to you?

6. **Woman:** Someplace with some entertainment. Also, I like the idea of cooking out on the beach a couple of times.

7. **Man:** That appeals to me too.

Part B.

For each phrase or sentence you indicated on the opposite page, rewrite that specific phrase or sentence in "I" language.

1. Man: _____

_____

2. Woman: _____

_____

3. Man: _____

_____

4. Woman: _____

_____

5. Man: _____

_____

6. Woman: _____

_____

7. Man: _____

_____

Part A.

Below, we have indicated instances we identified as not being "I" language. Don't be concerned if your responses are slightly different.

COMMENTARY

1. Man: *What would you like to do on our vacation?*

He asks a question without making his intentions clear.

2. Woman: *I don't know. What would you like to do?*

She indicates that she doesn't know, when she actually does have some ideas as indicated later in the conversation.

3. Man: I'd like to be perfectly frank about what I want and I'd like to hear what you honestly want instead of fooling around with "I don't know — what do you want."

He uses "I" language to express his wants.

4. Woman: Okay, I'd like to go somewhere tropical where I can lie in the sun and watch people.

She uses "I" language to state her wants.

5. Man: I'm not interested in lying in the sun, but I would like to play some sports like volleyball, racquetball, tennis, et cetera. That could be tropical. *What kind of night life appeals to you?*

This question is asked before he states his preference. Don't be concerned if you didn't catch this one.

6. Woman: Someplace with some entertainment. Also, I like the idea of cooking out on the beach a couple of times.

She's still using "I" language.

7. Man: That appeals to me too.

"That" is acceptable here because he's talking about himself and what he likes.

Part B.

Below, we have rewritten the phrases and sentences indicated on the previous page in "I" language. Your answers may differ so if you're in doubt, check them against the definition to ensure that you have used "I" language.

1. **Man:** I'd like to start making vacation plans and I was wondering what you wanted to do.

2. **Woman:** Let me think and while I'm thinking, I'd like to hear where you want to go and what you want to do.

3. **Man:**

4. **Woman:**

5. **Man:** I'd like to have our evenings somewhat simple and inexpensive so we can stay longer. What are your thoughts?

6. **Woman:**

7. **Man:**

PRACTICE 5

Part A.

Underline or highlight wherever "I" language is *not* used.

1. **Woman:** Are you in a good mood?

2. **Man:** Why? What have you done now?

3. **Woman:** I went grocery shopping.

4. **Man:** What are the damages?

5. **Woman:** One hundred and twenty dollars.

6. **Man:** One hundred and twenty dollars!! You must think I'm made of money.

7. **Woman:** Whatever you're made of, you've got to eat.

8. **Man:** Your idea of eating is lobster and filet mignon. You never think about economy, do you?

9. **Woman:** Yes I do, but you never think about quality.

10. **Man:** Why can't you combine the two?

11. **Woman:** Why don't you just do it yourself from now on?

Part B.

For each phrase or sentence you indicated on the opposite page, rewrite that specific phrase or sentence in "I" language.

1. **Woman:** _____
   _____

2. **Man:** _____
   _____

3. **Woman:** _____
   _____

4. **Man:** _____
   _____

5. **Woman:** _____
   _____

6. **Man:** _____
   _____

7. **Woman:** _____
   _____

8. **Man:** _____
   _____

9. **Woman:** _____
   _____

10. **Man:** _____
    _____

11. **Woman:** _____
    _____

Part A.

Below, we have indicated instances we identified as *not* being "I" language. Don't be concerned if your responses are slightly different.

COMMENTARY

1. Woman: *Are you in a good mood?*

She asks a question without stating her feelings first.

2. Man: *Why? What have you done now?*

With another question, he represents his opinion that she has done something wrong.

3. Woman: I went grocery shopping.

No comment.

4. Man: *What are the damages?*

He gets suspicious of her motives for asking the question and comes back with a question representing his opinion that she's spent too much.

5. Woman: One hundred and twenty dollars.

No comment.

6. Man: One hundred and twenty dollars!! *You must think* I'm made of money.

Using "you" he talks about what she thinks.

7. Woman: Whatever you're made of, *you've got* to eat.

Using "have to" she tells him about what his obligation is. She also uses "you" in talking about his behavior.

8. Man: *Your idea* of eating is lobster and filet mignon. *You never think about economy, do you?*

Using "you" he talks about her feelings and generalizes about what she'll **never** do. He uses a question to express his opinion.

9. Woman: Yes I do, but *you never think* about quality.

She generalizes about what he will **never** do.

10. Man: *Why can't you combine the two?*

He uses a question instead of expressing his opinion that he'd like her to combine quality and economy. He is also asking her **why** she behaves the way she does.

11. Woman: *Why don't you just do it yourself from now on?*

She uses a question to hide her opinion — that she is uncomfortable doing the grocery shopping when she has to face so much criticism.

Part B.

Below, we have rewritten the phrases and sentences indicated on the previous page in "I" language. Your answers may differ so if you're in doubt, check them against the definition to ensure that you have used "I" language.

1. **Woman:** I have some bad news. I'm hoping you're in a good mood.

2. **Man:** Oh! What is it?

3. **Woman:**

4. **Man:** I see. I guess the bad news is that you spent a lot of money. Is that it?

5. **Woman:**

6. **Man:** I'm really distressed by that amount.

7. **Woman:** (This cannot really be said in "I" language.)

8. **Man:** I'm really concerned about economizing.

9. **Woman:** I am too, but I like to get quality for my money as well.

10. **Man:** I wonder if it's possible to combine the two.

11. **Woman:** I wouldn't mind you taking it over if you like.

CHAPTER 6

IDENTIFYING DEFENSIVENESS

INTRODUCTION

DEFENSIVENESS IS a very powerful and destructive secondary emotion. More often than any other, it blocks effective communication because a person who is feeling defensive is usually unable to express any primary feelings in "I" language. For this reason, it is important that you be alert for signs of defensiveness in yourself.

Monitoring your own behavior can help you avoid expressing yourself defensively. It can also aid you in determining when you're not able to curb your defensiveness. This is important to know since it is best to discontinue a conversation when you feel unable to express your primary feelings. Often your defensiveness can be a clue to deeper emotions that you haven't been aware of.

Monitoring your partner's behavior can help you determine when he or she is out of control. Of course, you'll want to check this out with your partner rather than just assume he or she is out of control. It is best to state your concerns and ask if your partner wants to continue. Sometimes your partner's defensiveness can alert you to poor use or nonuse of "I" language on your part.

GOAL

We want you to be able to readily recognize defensiveness in yourself so you'll be better able to avoid it. In this chapter, you'll be taking the first steps toward that goal. Given a conversation in which one individual is behaving defensively during at least part of the conversation, you will be asked to identify those statements that indicate defensiveness.

DEFINITION

Defensiveness may be indicated whenever you hear yourself:

1. Talking in an angry, sarcastic, or resentful tone of voice.
2. Accusing or name-calling.
3. Blaming or faultfinding.
4. Assuming you have been blamed for or accused of something.
5. Interpreting motives for behavior you observe in your partner.

 # ELABORATION

When you are feeling or behaving defensively, it is usually because you are protecting rather than expressing your primary feelings. You are probably feeling hurt or afraid, and defensiveness is an attempt to avoid being hurt further. It is important to recognize when you are behaving defensively because defensiveness prevents constructive communication.

Recognizing Defensiveness

Many times you will recognize your defensiveness simply because you *feel* defensive. But at other times you may find yourself speaking defensively before you are aware of your feelings. Here are some things to listen for that can warn you that you're expressing yourself defensively.

1. Talking in an Angry, Sarcastic, or Resentful Tone of Voice

Your tone of voice carries your message as much as the words you choose. It is often the easiest sign of defensiveness to recognize. Anytime you hear yourself speaking angrily or resentfully, you need to check out your primary feelings. A sarcastic tone of voice may indicate that you are saying hurtful things to your partner. It is not unusual for a defensive person to try to protect himself or herself by striking out at others.

An angry tone of voice does not always indicate defensiveness, but check it out to be sure.

2. Accusing or Name-Calling

One of the most destructive ways to protect yourself from being hurt is to take the offensive and attack the other person. Here are some typical accusations made out of defensiveness:

You're totally insensitive and irresponsible.

You're just like my mother.

You're seeing someone else, aren't you.

You don't know anything about love or sex.

As for name-calling, most people have seen, heard, or used quite a number of the names people call each other when they're angry or defensive.

3. Blaming or Faultfinding

Blaming or faultfinding is similar to making accusations and name-calling because it involves striking out at others to protect yourself. Here are some typical statements.

It's all your fault.

You have only yourself to blame.

You're making me upset and angry.

I'm depressed because of what you did.

4. Assuming You've Been Blamed for or Accused of Something

Frequently, while on the defensive, an individual may take everything the other person says as an accusation or blame. This can occur even when the other person is making every attempt to use "I" language and express primary feelings. Below are some two-line conversations that show what we mean. The first line is in "I" language and the second line is a defensive response.

"I" Language: I'm going to straighten this room a little bit.

Defensive Response: You think I'm a lousy housekeeper. Is that it?

"I" Language: I'm really upset that I can't find those papers.

Defensive Response: I suppose you're blaming me for losing them!

"I" Language: I'd like to try something new next time we have intercourse.

Defensive Response: Oh, so you think I'm boring in bed.

5. Interpreting Motives for Behavior You Observe in Your Partner

Feeling defensive often leads to misinterpreting the motives and intentions of people you love. This can really hurt somebody who is trying to communicate effectively and be open with their feelings. Here are some examples of what we mean:

You're just trying to get your own way like you always do.

You're trying to trap me.

You're trying to get out of going to bed with me.

You don't really love me, do you.

Not Using "I" Language or Expressing Primary Feelings

You've probably noticed in the statements we've given as examples that "I" language is not used in any of them, nor are primary feelings expressed. This might serve as one of the best additional warnings to you when you are speaking defensively.

SAMPLE CONVERSATIONS

FOLLOWING ARE four sample conversations. In each, defensiveness can be seen in the behavior of one individual. Statements that may be interpreted as defensive are indicated in the conversation. In the commentary are remarks about each statement. Read through only as many sample conversations as you feel you need to be able to recognize defensiveness.

NOTE:

As in previous chapters, we'll be evaluating what other people say in the examples and practice. Ideally, you need to evaluate your own behavior and communication. You may think your partner is becoming defensive, but it is essential that you check it out with him or her.

Sample Conversation 1

In the conversation below, defensiveness can be observed in the behavior of the woman speaking. Defensive statements are indicated by bold italics and discussed in the commentary.

COMMENTARY

Man: Honey, I'm getting very concerned about our son's behavior. He seems undisciplined lately and sort of willful.

He states his concerns, using "I" language.

Woman: I agree, but I'm not sure what to do about it.

She responds in "I" language.

Man: Well, I'm not home all day so I don't know how you relate to him, but I'd like to be firmer with him. I let him get away with all sorts of things that really bother me. He's starting to take advantage of me.

He talks about what he wants, in "I" language.

Woman: So *you think I'm not firm enough with him.*

She's assuming that he has accused her of not being firm enough. She's speaking in an irritated tone of voice.

Man: I didn't mean to imply that. Only you would know about that.

He tries to clarify his meaning.

Woman: *Well, I think I'm a very good mother and that he's a pretty good boy for his age.*

She's speaking resentfully. It sounds as though she thinks she's been accused of being an unfit mother.

Man: I do, too, but I don't want him to learn that he can have his way all the time at somebody else's expense.

He talks about what he wants, in "I" language.

Woman: *Oh, I get it, you think this is all my problem; that I'm entirely too lax with him and that I let him do anything he wants.*

She's misinterpreting his motives and accusing him. She's also speaking sarcastically.

Man: I was really only talking about how I treat him....

He tries to clarify his meaning.

Woman: *Well, that's all you know isn't it? After all, you don't have to spend all day, every day, with him. I just don't have the time or energy to be the perfect mother all the time.*

She's speaking angrily and continues to think he's attacking her.

136

Sample Conversation 2

In the conversation below, defensiveness can be observed in the behavior of the man speaking. Defensive statements are indicated by bold italics and discussed in the commentary.

COMMENTARY

Woman: I'm planning to buy a new dress for the dinner party. Do you have any objections?

She states her intentions before asking a question — good "I" language.

Man: We have the money, but I don't know why you need a new dress.

He's implying that she doesn't need a new dress by using "why" — not "I" language.

Woman: I don't actually need a new dress. I want a new dress and the reason is just that it makes me feel good to have a new dress.

She talks about her desires, in "I" language.

Man: I don't buy clothes because I want them; I buy them because I need them.

He uses "I" language.

Woman: I understand that. I'm glad this came up because I would like for you to understand or at least accept my feelings about having new clothes.

She talks about what she wants, in "I" language.

Man: ***You make me feel like Scrooge.***

He's irritated and blaming her for making him feel like Scrooge.

Woman: That wasn't my intention. I'd just like to avoid having this same discussion about why I need new clothes next time I want to buy something.

She tries to clarify her meaning, in "I" language.

Man: ***You can't change the way I am.***

He's misinterpreting her motives.

Woman: I'm not trying to change the way you are. I'm not criticizing your feelings about clothes; I just want my feelings to be respected and accepted.

She's still trying to clarify her feelings and desires.

Man: ***Go and buy whatever you want. I'm not going to be the heavy and say no. I certainly wouldn't want to deprive you.***

He's speaking angrily and sarcastically.

Sample Conversation 3

In the conversation below, defensiveness can be observed in the behavior of the woman speaking.

COMMENTARY

Man: You seem troubled. Is there anything wrong?

He uses good "I" language by stating his concern and then asking her to respond.

Woman: I'm just depressed; that's all. *I suppose you want to know why.*

She's probably speaking in a sarcastic tone of voice indicating defensiveness.

Man: I'm interested.

He expresses his feeling, in "I" language.

Woman: Well, I'm not going to tell you. *You'll just think it's stupid.*

She assumes he'll think her depression is stupid, indicating defensiveness on her part.

Man: Look, I don't mind if you don't tell me, but I'm not going to think you're stupid.

He tries to clarify his feelings, using "I" language.

Woman: I'm depressed because I planned all week to lie in the sun today and it was overcast all day. *See, I told you it was dumb.*

She's still assuming he thinks she's dumb.

Man: I don't think it's dumb. It bothers me that you assume I'm not going to understand.

He's still trying to clarify how he feels in "I" language.

Woman: *You never get depressed. How could you understand?*

She's making defensive accusations.

Man: I do get depressed. I'm getting depressed right now.

He's getting frustrated, but still uses "I" language.

Woman: I guess I've been too defensive. I'm always worried that you'll think I'm silly or weak.

She finally expresses her feelings in "I" language.

138

Sample Conversation 4

In the conversation below, defensiveness can be observed in the behavior of the woman speaking.

COMMENTARY

Man: Honey, next time we make love, I'd like to see you in that sexy nightgown I bought you.

He's using "I" language to express his desires.

Woman: *Why?*

She sounds suspicious and defensive.

Man: So I can take it off you. I think I would find it arousing.

He's continuing to use "I" language.

Woman: *You must be pretty tired of me if you've got to do a dumb thing like that to make sex interesting.*

She's assuming that he's tired of her, indicating defensiveness on her part.

Man: I'm not tired of you, but I do like to try new things.

He tries to clarify his feelings, using "I" language.

Woman: *Why don't you just try a new woman? I'm sure that would be exciting for you.,*

She's still defensive and assuming that he's tired and bored with her.

Man: I get the feeling that you're upset about this. Are you?

He uses "I" language, stating his concern first and then asking her to respond.

Woman: *Me upset? No, I like to be told I'm a sexual bore.*

She's speaking sarcastically, indicating that she's still feeling defensive.

Man: I am not bored by you. I'd like to discuss this later if you don't mind. I'm feeling a little upset myself.

He's become frustrated, but still expresses himself in "I" language.

PRACTICE

FOLLOWING ARE four practice sets. For each, there is a conversation like the ones in the sample conversation section. You are to underline or highlight the statements in the conversation that indicate defensiveness. On the facing page, there are spaces for you to give your reasons. As in the sample conversations, only one individual is behaving defensively in each conversation. Look at the feedback on the pages following each item immediately after completing the item. If you feel you've done well on the first couple of items, go on to the next chapter. If you have trouble with the practice, go back and review the definition, the elaboration, and the sample conversations. Then try the practice items again.

Part A.

Study the sample conversation below and determine which statements indicate defensiveness. Underline or highlight those statements. You can assume that only one of the individuals is speaking defensively.

1. **Man:** This magazine has nude men in it. I never knew you liked this garbage.

2. **Woman:** I haven't liked any magazines till this one. I find it much more tasteful and kind of classy.

3. **Man:** You don't find these men attractive, do you?

4. **Woman:** A little, but only physically.

5. **Man:** I didn't realize that you weren't physically attracted to me. I always thought I was good-looking.

6. **Woman:** You are, silly. I've always been attracted to you. In fact, that's one of the reasons I fell in love with you. But, I find these men attractive too.

7. **Man:** Well, you're no great beauty either. I find other women more attractive too.

8. **Woman:** I'm sorry you feel this way. I'm not comparing these men to you and I do find you very attractive. I'd like to talk about this more, because I'm worried that you're jealous.

9. **Man:** Well, I guess I am, a little. I've just always been afraid you'll find someone more attractive than me.

Part B.

For each of the statements you indicated on the facing page, explain briefly why you think it is defensive.

1. Man: _____

_____

2. Woman: _____

_____

3. Man: _____

_____

4. Woman: _____

_____

5. Man: _____

_____

6. Woman: _____

_____

7. Man: _____

_____

8. Woman: _____

_____

9. Man: _____

_____

Part A.

Below, we have indicated those statements we feel are defensive in bold italics.

1. **Man:** This magazine has nude men in it. *I never knew you liked this garbage.*

2. **Woman:** I haven't liked any magazines till this one. I find it much more tasteful and kind of classy.

3. **Man:** *You don't find these men attractive, do you?*

4. **Woman:** A little, but only physically.

5. **Man:** *I didn't realize that you weren't physically attracted to me. I always thought I was good-looking.*

6. **Woman:** You are, silly. I've always been attracted to you. In fact, that's one of the reasons I fell in love with you. But, I find these men attractive too.

7. **Man:** *Well, you're no great beauty either. I find other women more attractive too.*

8. **Woman:** I'm sorry you feel this way. I'm not comparing these men to you and I do find you very attractive. I'd like to talk about this more, because I'm worried that you're jealous.

9. **Man:** Well, I guess I am, a little. I've just always been afraid you'll find someone more attractive than me.

Part B.

For each of the statements indicated in the conversation, we have explained why we feel it is defensive. Your reasons may be somewhat different.

1. **Man:** He's being sarcastic. Don't be concerned if you missed this one.

2. **Woman:** She's expressing her opinion, using "I" language.

3. **Man:** He's still being sarcastic.

4. **Woman:** No comment.

5. **Man:** He's assuming that she isn't attracted to him, and that that is why she's reading the magazine.

6. **Woman:** She's expressing herself in "I" language.

7. **Man;** He's name-calling and being sarcastic.

8. **Woman:** She's still using "I" language.

9. **Man:** He finally begins to use "I" language and to express his feelings.

PRACTICE 2

Part A.

Study the sample conversation below and determine which statements indicate defensiveness. Underline or highlight those statements. You can assume that only one of the individuals involved is speaking defensively.

1. **Woman:** I'd like to know why you get so upset every time we go to a party together.

2. **Man:** I get uncomfortable when I see you talking with other men.

3. **Woman:** Why are you so jealous?

4. **Man:** I don't know. I guess I feel a little insecure.

5. **Woman:** You don't trust me, do you?

6. **Man:** No, that's not it at all. I trust you, but I get these other feelings too.

7. **Woman:** Well, I guess we'd better not go to any more parties if you're always going to be so sensitive.

Part B.

For each of the statements you indicated on the facing page, explain briefly why you think it is defensive.

1. **Woman:** _____

   _____

2. **Man:** _____

   _____

3. **Woman:** _____

   _____

4. **Man:** _____

   _____

5. **Woman:** _____

   _____

6. **Man:** _____

   _____

7. **Woman:** _____

   _____

FEEDBACK 2

Part A.

Below, we have indicated those statements we feel are defensive in bold italics.

1. **Woman:** *I'd like to know why you get so upset every time we go to a party together.*

2. **Man:** I get uncomfortable when I see you talking with other men.

3. **Woman:** *Why are you so jealous?*

4. **Man:** I don't know. I guess I feel a little insecure.

5. **Woman:** *You don't trust me, do you?*

6. **Man:** No, that's not it at all. I trust you, but I get these other feelings too.

7. **Woman:** *Well, I guess we'd better not go to any more parties if you're always going to be so sensitive.*

Part B.

For each of the statements indicated in the conversation, we have explained why we feel it is defensive. Your reasons may be somewhat different.

1. **Woman:** She's assuming he's upset and she sounds very defensive.

2. **Man:** He expresses his feelings, in "I" language.

3. **Woman:** She's accusing him of jealousy, indicating defensiveness on her part.

4. **Man:** He's still expressing his feelings, in "I" language.

5. **Woman:** She's still making defensive accusations.

6. **Man:** He tries to clarify his meaning, using "I" language.

7. **Woman:** She's still too defensive to hear what he's saying.

PRACTICE 3

Part A.

Study the sample conversation below and determine which statements indicate defensiveness. Underline or highlight those statements. You can assume that only one of the individuals involved is speaking defensively.

1. **Woman:** I'm going to play in the neighborhood game next weekend and I'd love to have your company.

2. **Man:** No, I'm no good at softball.

3. **Woman:** I don't think anyone else is, either. It's probably just for fun. I think I'll sign up.

4. **Man:** Is that supposed to be a challenge?

5. **Woman:** Challenge? No, I just think I'd have fun. I don't expect you to do it. I'd like it if you came to watch me.

6. **Man:** Oh, sure. My wife the jock. I know you think I'm not very athletic for a man.

7. **Woman:** Look, I know you don't like sports that much, but I'm not bothered by it. I wish you'd believe that.

8. **Man:** Well, it's something I'm very sensitive about.

9. **Woman:** I understand that, but I'd be unhappy to think you were feeling pressured by me.

10. **Man:** So, I'll come watch.

Part B.

For each of the statements you indicated on the facing page, explain briefly why you think it is defensive.

1. Woman: _____

_____

2. Man: _____

_____

3. Woman: _____

_____

4. Man: _____

_____

5. Woman: _____

_____

6. Man: _____

_____

7. Woman: _____

_____

8. Man: _____

_____

9. Woman: _____

_____

10. Man: _____

_____

FEEDBACK 3

Part A.

Below, we have indicated those statements we feel are defensive in bold italics.

1. **Woman:** I'm going to play in the neighborhood game next weekend and I'd love to have your company.

2. **Man:** No, I'm no good at softball.

3. **Woman:** I don't think anyone else is, either. It's probably just for fun. I think I'll sign up.

4. **Man:** *Is that supposed to be a challenge?*

5. **Woman:** Challenge? No, I just think I'd have fun. I don't expect you to do it. I'd like it if you came to watch me.

6. **Man:** *Oh, sure. My wife the jock. I know you think I'm not very athletic for a man.*

7. **Woman:** Look, I know you don't like sports that much, but I'm not bothered by it. I wish you'd believe that.

8. **Man:** Well, it's something I'm very sensitive about.

9. **Woman:** I understand that, but I'd be unhappy to think you were feeling pressured by me.

10. **Man:** So, I'll come watch.

Part B.

For each of the statements indicated in the conversation, we have explained why we feel it is defensive. Your reasons may be somewhat different.

1. **Woman:** She states her desires clearly — good "I" language.

2. **Man:** No comment.

3. **Woman:** No comment.

4. **Man:** He's assumed that she's challenged him and is speaking defensively.

5. **Woman:** She tries to clarify her meaning.

6. **Man:** He's speaking sarcastically and defensively. He's assuming that she thinks badly of him for not being athletic.

7. **Woman:** She tries again to clarify her meaning, using "I" language.

8. **Man:** He finally uses "I" language to express his feelings.

9. **Woman:** She's using "I" language.

10. **Man:** Apparently he's overcome his defensiveness.

PRACTICE 4

Part A.

Study the sample conversation below and determine which statements indicate defensiveness. Underline or highlight those statements. You can assume that only one of the individuals involved is speaking defensively.

1. **Man:** I'm very upset about something concerning our checkbook. I'd like to discuss it with you.

2. **Woman:** Okay, what is it?

3. **Man:** Well, I looked in our checkbook just now and there are three checks with no amounts.

4. **Woman:** Naturally, you think I'm responsible.

5. **Man:** Well, I don't remember writing these checks myself, but I was going to *ask* you about it, not accuse you.

6. **Woman:** Oh sure. Even if I said "No," you wouldn't believe me for a minute.

7. **Man:** I'm hurt that you think that.

8. **Woman:** You're just saying that to make me confess. Well, I won't talk.

9. **Man:** I'm not trying to weasel a confession out of you. I'm more interested in figuring out what the amounts are so I know where our account stands.

10. **Woman:** You mean you just wanted to know if I did it in case I remembered the amount?

11. **Man:** That's it.

12. **Woman:** I'm sorry I misunderstood you. Actually, I remember writing two of the checks. Maybe I can figure out what the amounts were.

Part B.

For each of the statements you indicated on the facing page, explain briefly why you think it is defensive.

1. Man: _____
_____

2. Woman: _____
_____

3. Man: _____
_____

4. Woman: _____
_____

5. Man: _____
_____

6. Woman: _____
_____

7. Man: _____
_____

8. Woman: _____
_____

9. Man: _____
_____

10. Woman: _____
_____

11. Man: _____
_____

12. Woman: _____
_____

Part A.

Below, we have indicated those statements we feel are defensive in bold italics.

1. **Man:** I'm very upset about something concerning our checkbook. I'd like to discuss it with you.

2. **Woman:** Okay, what is it?

3. **Man:** Well, I looked in our checkbook just now and there are three checks with no amounts.

4. **Woman:** *Naturally, you think I'm responsible.*

5. **Man:** Well, I don't remember writing these checks myself, but I was going to *ask* you about it, not accuse you.

6. **Woman:** *Oh sure. Even if I said "No," you wouldn't believe me for a minute.*

7. **Man:** I'm hurt that you think that.

8. **Woman:** *You're just saying that to make me confess. Well, I won't talk.*

9. **Man:** I'm not trying to weasel a confession out of you. I'm more interested in figuring out what the amounts are so we know where our account stands.

10. **Woman:** You mean you just wanted to know if I did it in case I remembered the amount?

11. **Man:** That's it.

12. **Woman:** I'm sorry I misunderstood you. Actually, I remember writing two of the checks. Maybe I can figure out what the amounts were.

Part B.

For each of the statements indicated in the conversation, we have explained why we feel it is defensive. Your reasons may be somewhat different.

1. **Man:**   He uses "I" language to express his concerns and desires.

2. **Woman:** No comment.

3. **Man:**   No comment.

4. **Woman:** She's assuming that he has blamed her.

5. **Man:**   He tries to clarify his intentions, using "I" language.

6. **Woman:** She's assuming that he won't believe her. She's misinterpreting his motives.

7. **Man:**   He expresses his feelings, in "I" language.

8. **Woman:** She's sarcastically accusing him of trying to make her confess.

9. **Man:**   He tries again to clarify his intentions, using "I" language.

10. **Woman:** She begins to hear what he's saying.

11. **Man:**   No comment.

12. **Woman:** She uses "I" language.

CHAPTER 7

IDENTIFYING VULNERABILITY

INTRODUCTION

YOU ALREADY know how important it is to express primary feelings as much as possible, and you've probably realized how vulnerable and defenseless this can leave you. But as undesirable as it sounds, defenselessness is far more constructive than defensiveness. You've already seen the hurtful effects of defensiveness in the previous chapter. In an emotional confrontation, partners can avoid this destructive trap by choosing to be vulnerable and open, each trusting the other not to take advantage of his or her vulnerability. As long as this trust and willingness to be open exists, constructive communication can continue. When either individual becomes defensive, it's time to re-evaluate the situation. If one partner is feeling defensive and finds it too difficult to remain vulnerable, the interaction needs to be discontinued for the time being until *both* individuals are willing and able to make themselves vulnerable and express their primary feelings openly.

GOAL

We want you to be able to identify vulnerability in yourself and in your partner. In this chapter, you will be taking the first step toward that goal. You'll be given a conversation and asked to identify those statements that indicate vulnerability.

DEFINITION

A statement indicates vulnerability when you are:

1. Expressing primary feelings in "I" language.

2. Taking an emotional risk.

3. Avoiding defensiveness.

 # ELABORATION

It is very important that you are able to identify vulnerable statements so you can demonstrate your willingness to be vulnerable, as well as recognize when others are being vulnerable. Below, we'll describe in more detail the three points in the definition.

1. Expressing Primary Feelings in "I" Language

Whenever you express your primary feelings, you are making yourself vulnerable by being open and honest about some of your deepest emotions. As we have said so many times before, this openness is critical in exercising self-responsibility and in effectively communicating with those you love. Using "I" language to express primary feelings contributes to your vulnerability because it means you are accepting responsibility for your feelings.

2. Taking an Emotional Risk

Expressing primary feelings can be emotionally risky, particularly when the person you're dealing with is angry or defensive. He or she is more likely to hurt you when feeling this way. The risk is often well worth taking though, because the more open *you* are, the more comfortable your partner will feel in expressing his or her primary feelings. Sometimes you will feel willing to take the risk because you feel it is in your best interest. Other times you may be feeling too tired, or sick, or fragile to risk being vulnerable. You may decide at any time during a conversation that you are no longer willing to take the risk. In any instance where you feel emotionally unprepared to be vulnerable, it is a good idea to consider discontinuing the conversation until you do feel prepared.

It is also important to recognize when your partner is being vulnerable because it would be so easy to hurt him or her. For instance, you may be feeling angry and defensive while your partner is trying to express his or her primary feelings. In anger, you may fail to recognize this vulnerability and respond hurtfully. This is to be avoided, whenever possible, because it is very destructive.

3. Avoiding Defensiveness

Sometimes being vulnerable means that in a situation in which you feel very defensive, you actively choose *not* to express yourself defensively. This is a difficult position to take, as it represents an emotional risk and often takes quite a bit of emotional energy.

SAMPLE
CONVERSATIONS

O N THE following pages are four conversations in which the individuals make statements showing vulnerability. In each conversation, these statements are indicated. In the commentary you'll find remarks for each statement. Study only as many conversations as you need to be able to identify vulnerability.

Sample Conversation 1

In the conversation below, the statements showing vulnerability are indicated by bold italics.

		COMMENTARY
Man:	Hey, your hair is different. Come closer so I can see.	No comment.
Woman:	I didn't ask you before I did it because I knew you'd say no.	She's sounding defensive.
Man:	***It's your hair. I have my preferences, but I want you to be happy with it too.***	He's trying to assure her there's no need for her to be defensive.
Woman:	You don't like it, I can tell.	She's still defensive.
Man:	Frankly, ***I haven't made up my mind yet. I think I like it.***	He's taking something of a risk in admitting that he's not sure how he feels about her hair.
Woman:	Well, it'll be too bad if you don't. I can't change it now.	She's becoming even more defensive.
Man:	You know, I'm getting kind of annoyed. I am concerned that you've already made up your mind that I'll be mad and won't like it. ***I'm hurt by that.***	He's stating his primary feelings of hurt and, therefore, making himself vulnerable.
Woman:	***Well, I guess I was just so afraid you wouldn't like that I cut it.*** You used to tell me so often how much you liked it the other way.	She's finally stopped being defensive and is expressing her primary feelings of fear.
Man:	I did, but I may very well decide I like it this way. ***At any rate, I'd like to feel you were happy with it whether I liked it or not.***	He is expressing vulnerability by indicating that her happiness with her appearance is a priority for him.

In the conversation below, the statements showing vulnerability are indicated by bold italics.

COMMENTARY

Woman: I'm awfully tired. I'm going to bed.

No comment.

Man: I was just thinking about going to bed myself, but for a different reason. I feel like making love. Are you too tired for that?

He expresses his desires using "I" language. Also, he's stated his intentions before asking a question.

Woman: Yes, I'm afraid I am.

She responds.

Man: *I'm beginning to feel really neglected. I'd like to find a way to set aside some time for us to be together intimately. How do you feel about that?*

He's expressing his primary feelings in "I" language.

Woman: You're saying I'm always tired or have some other excuse.

She's assuming that he's accused her of making excuses.

Man: No, I'm just trying to find a solution that will work for both of us. *I want to make love to you more often than we do now. I get to feeling very frustrated after a while.*

He's continuing to express his primary feelings even though she's become defensive. This represents somewhat of a risk for him.

Woman: You're a typical man. Only interested in sex.

She's making accusations.

Man: I'm interested in more than sex. *I like being close to you.*

He's still expressing his primary feelings, even though the emotional risk is greater.

Woman: I don't know why you're making me feel so guilty about this.

She's accusing him of trying to make her feel guilty.

Sample Conversation 3

In the conversation below, the statements showing vulnerability are indicated.

COMMENTARY

Woman: I have a real problem with your clothes in the morning. I like our bedroom to be neat, and it can't be until I've picked up your clothes. Would you be interested in helping me out?

She expresses her feelings and wants in "I" language.

Man: You're saying I'm a slob.

He's assuming that she's accused him of being a slob.

Woman: No, I'm not. I'm asking if you'd be willing to help me solve my problem.

She tries to clarify her meaning using "I" language.

Man: You're just like my mother, only sneakier. She always tried to get me to pick up my things, only she was a lot more straightforward.

He accuses her of trying to coerce him.

Woman: You think I'm trying to coerce you?

She asks about his feelings rather than accusing him.

Man: Sure, what happens if I say "No"? Then you'll start yelling, and nagging, and trying to make me feel guilty.

He's speaking defensively.

Woman: Since it's my problem, if you say no, I'll just have to handle it myself. After all, I can't force you to pick up your clothes.

She talks about her feelings, using "I" language.

Man: *You mean you wouldn't try to make me feel guilty?*

He's beginning to overcome his defensiveness.

Woman: *No. I'm hurt that you think I'd do that.*

She's expressing her primary feelings in "I" language and taking a small risk in doing so.

Man: *I'd like to start this conversation over. I think I've been unnecessarily defensive.*

He has overcome his defensiveness and appears ready to express his primary feelings in "I" language.

168

In the conversation below, the statements showing vulnerability are indicated.

COMMENTARY

Man: Yuck!

No comment.

Woman: What's the matter?

No comment.

Man: I think these tomatoes must be two months old. They're absolutely rotten.

No comment.

Woman: I must have forgotten about them.

No comment.

Man: Honey, I get really bugged when I find rotting food in the refrigerator. I get queasy.

He expresses his feelings, using "I" language.

Woman: So that makes me a lousy housekeeper, I suppose.

She's assuming that he's accused her of being a lousy housekeeper. This indicates defensiveness on her part.

Man: *No, but I guess it bothers me more than you. It's my problem. I'd just like to find a way to avoid it.*

He's making himself vulnerable by expressing his feelings in "I" language.

Woman: Don't look in the refrigerator.

She's speaking sarcastically.

Man: *I'm serious about finding a solution, but I'd be willing to discuss it at another time. I didn't mean to offend you.*

He's still being vulnerable, expressing his feelings in "I" language and avoiding defensiveness. This represents an emotional risk, since she is behaving so defensively.

Woman: *Well, I feel really inadequate, like I'm a bad wife not doing my duty.*

She finally expresses her primary feelings in "I" language, overcoming her defensiveness to do so.

Man: I'm not saying it's your duty, and I'm not saying it's your fault.

He clarifies his meaning, using "I" language. This could be a statement showing vulnerability, even though we did not indicate it as such.

Woman: *In that case, I feel better about discussing it.*

She expresses her feelings using "I" language. She's being vulnerable by choosing to take the emotional risk of starting the conversation over again.

169

PRACTICE

FOLLOWING ARE four practice items. Each presents a sample conversation. You are to study the conversation and then underline or highlight those statements you feel show vulnerability. Then, for each statement you indicated, explain why you thought it showed vulnerability. After completing each item, look at the feedback on the following pages. If you feel you did well on the first couple of items, go on to the next chapter. If you have trouble with any of the items, go back and review the definition, the elaboration, and the sample conversations. Then try the practice again.

Part A.

Study the sample conversation below, and indicate those statements you feel show vulnerability.

1. **Woman:** I'd like to take you to dinner tonight. What do you think about that?

2. **Man:** It's not my birthday. What are you up to?

3. **Woman:** Well, I've been complaining a lot lately that you never take me anywhere, so I decided to do something instead of complain. I feel that I've been unfair.

4. **Man:** Sounds fishy to me.

5. **Woman:** I get the feeling you're suspicious of my motives. Is that right?

6. **Man:** Well, yes, to tell you the truth. You have to admit this is quite a switch in your tactics.

7. **Woman:** I'm sorry you feel that way. I'd like you to believe that I'm honestly sorry about my actions. I feel it's a mistake for me to just expect you always to be the one to take me out.

8. **Man:** Well, I was feeling kind of pressured about it. I like taking you out; but when I feel you expect it, I feel taken for granted.

9. **Woman:** I know that. So I want to invite you out. My treat.

Part B.

For each statement you indicated, write why you think it shows vulnerability.

1. **Woman:** _____

   _____

2. **Man:** _____

   _____

3. **Woman:** _____

   _____

4. **Man:** _____

   _____

5. **Woman:** _____

   _____

6. **Man:** _____

   _____

7. **Woman:** _____

   _____

8. **Man:** _____

   _____

9. **Woman:** _____

   _____

Part A.

Below, we have indicated those statements we feel show vulnerability in bold italics.

1. **Woman:** I'd like to take you to dinner tonight. What do you think about that?

2. **Man:** It's not my birthday. What are you up to?

3. **Woman:** Well, I've been complaining a lot lately that you never take me anywhere, so I decided to do something instead of complain. *I feel that I've been unfair.*

4. **Man:** Sounds fishy to me.

5. **Woman:** I get the feeling you're suspicious of my motives. Is that right?

6. **Man:** Well, yes, to tell you the truth. You have to admit this is quite a switch in your tactics.

7. **Woman:** I'm sorry you feel that way. *I'd like you to believe that I'm honestly sorry about my actions. I feel it's a mistake for me to just expect you always to be the one to take me out.*

8. **Man:** *Well, I was feeling kind of pressured about it. I like taking you out; but when I feel you expect it, I feel taken for granted.*

9. **Woman:** I know that. So I want to invite you out. My treat.

Part B.

For each statement we indicated, we've shown why we think it shows vulnerability.

1. **Woman:** She states her intentions before asking for a response from him — good "I" language.

2. **Man:** He's sounding a little suspicious and maybe defensive.

3. **Woman:** She is taking an emotional risk by admitting to a mistake and is implying an apology.

4. **Man:** He's still a bit resistant.

5. **Woman:** She states her concerns and asks him to confirm or deny.

6. **Man:** He's still resistant and suspicious.

7. **Woman:** She restates her apology in more detail, making herself more vulnerable. Also, she's avoiding becoming defensive herself, even though he is distrustful.

8. **Man:** He is finally expressing his primary feelings nondefensively.

9. **Woman:** You could have underlined these statements as indicating vulnerability, even though we did not.

Part A.

Study the sample conversation below, and indicate those statements you feel show vulnerability.

1. **Woman:** I read an article the other day that said impotence was mostly a state of mind. I'd like you to read it, so we could talk about it.

2. **Man:** I'm not a psychosomatic! How many times do I have to tell you that?

3. **Woman:** I only brought it up because I'm worried about you and I want to help. I love you, you know.

4. **Man:** I know you're trying to help, but I get so embarrassed talking about this problem with you that I get angry.

5. **Woman:** Well, it is my problem too. I'd really like for our sex life to be the way it used to be.

6. **Man:** Well, I guess you would. Why don't you just look for someone else to sleep with?

7. **Woman:** I don't think that would solve the problem since I'm interested in sleeping with you. Maybe I'm the problem.

8. **Man:** Yeah, you bug me about it too much. Just leave me alone, okay?

Part B.

For each statement you indicated, write why you think it shows vulnerability.

1. Woman: _____

_____

2. Man: _____

_____

3. Woman: _____

_____

4. Man: _____

_____

5. Woman: _____

_____

6. Man: _____

_____

7. Woman: _____

_____

8. Man: _____

_____

FEEDBACK 2

Part A.

Below, we have indicated those statements we feel show vulnerability in bold italics.

1. **Woman:** I read an article the other day that said impotence was mostly a state of mind. I'd like you to read it so we could talk about it.

2. **Man:** I'm not a psychosomatic! How many times do I have to tell you that?

3. **Woman:** *I only brought it up because I'm worried about you and I want to help you. I love you, you know.*

4. **Man:** *I know you're trying to help, but I get so embarrassed talking about this problem with you that I get angry.*

5. **Woman:** *Well, it is my problem too. I'd really like for our sex life to be the way it used to be.*

6. **Man:** Well, I guess you would. Why don't you just look for someone else to sleep with?

7. **Woman:** *I don't think that would solve the problem since I'm interested in sleeping with you. Maybe I'm the problem.*

8. **Man:** Yeah, you bug me about it too much. Just leave me alone, okay?

Part B.

For each statement we indicated, we've shown why we think it shows vulnerability.

1. **Woman:** She states her wishes, using "I" language.

2. **Man:** He's speaking defensively.

3. **Woman:** She's taking a risk by expressing her primary feelings. She's avoiding defensiveness.

4. **Man:** He's trying to overcome his defensiveness and is taking the risk of expressing his primary feelings.

5. **Woman:** You may or may not have underlined these statements. She's expressing primary feelings.

6. **Man:** He's speaking sarcastically and defensively.

7. **Woman:** She continues to resist becoming defensive and expresses her primary feelings in "I" language.

8. **Man:** He's still defensive.

Part A.

Study the sample conversation below, and indicate those statements you feel show vulnerability.

1. **Woman:** I called your office today and your secretary said you were out all afternoon. I was wondering where you were.

2. **Man:** I had a business appointment with Ellen Taylor.

3. **Woman:** You mean the designer, Ellen Taylor?

4. **Man:** Yes, I get the feeling that upsets you.

5. **Woman:** Well, she's so beautiful.

6. **Man:** Yes, she's very beautiful and very charming. I enjoy doing business with her agency because she's so cooperative.

7. **Woman:** Well, too bad we weren't all born with her good looks.

8. **Man:** You think I find her more appealing than you. Is that it?

9. **Woman:** It crossed my mind.

10. **Man:** Well, I'm hurt that you don't have more faith in me.

11. **Woman:** You can't deny that she's more beautiful and you just now raved about her charm. I'm not blind, you know. I can see how much you are attracted to her.

12. **Man:** Hold it. I'd be lying if I said I didn't find her attractive. But we have nothing more than a friendly business relationship. I'm not looking for anything more than that. I'd like you to believe that so you could feel comfortable about my meetings with her. I'd be unhappy if you felt threatened.

13. **Woman:** Actually, I do trust you. I guess maybe I just envy her beauty. I'd like to be that beautiful. I suppose I'm afraid because she's so much more beautiful than I am.

Part B.

For each statement you indicated, write why you think it shows vulnerability.

1. **Woman:** _____

    _____

2. **Man:** _____

    _____

3. **Woman:** _____

    _____

4. **Man:** _____

    _____

5. **Woman:** _____

    _____

6. **Man:** _____

    _____

7. **Woman:** _____

    _____

8. **Man:** _____

    _____

9. **Woman:** _____

    _____

10. **Man:** _____

    _____

11. **Woman:** _____

    _____

12. **Man:** _____

    _____

13. **Woman:** _____

    _____

Part A.

Below, we have indicated those statements we feel show vulnerability.

1. **Woman:** I called your office today and your secretary said you were out all afternoon. I was wondering where you were.

2. **Man:** I had a business appointment with Ellen Taylor.

3. **Woman:** You mean the designer, Ellen Taylor?

4. **Man:** Yes, I get the feeling that upsets you.

5. **Woman:** Well, she's so beautiful.

6. **Man:** Yes, she's very beautiful and very charming. I enjoy doing business with her agency because she's so cooperative.

7. **Woman:** Well, too bad we weren't all born with her good looks.

8. **Man:** You think I find her more appealing than you. Is that it?

9. **Woman:** It crossed my mind.

10. **Man:** *Well, I'm hurt that you don't have more faith in me.*

11. **Woman:** You can't deny that she's more beautiful and you just now raved about her charm. I'm not blind, you know. I can see how much you are attracted to her.

12. **Man:** Hold it. I'd be lying if I said I didn't find her attractive, but we have nothing more than a friendly business relationship. I'm not looking for anything more than that. *I'd like you to believe that so you could feel comfortable about my meetings with her. I'd be unhappy if you felt threatened.*

13. **Woman:** *Actually, I do trust you. I guess maybe I just envy her beauty. I'd like to be that beautiful. I suppose I'm afraid because she's so much more beautiful than I am.*

Part B.

For each statement we indicated, we've shown why we think it shows vulnerability.

1. **Woman:** No comment.

2. **Man:** No comment.

3. **Woman:** She sounds as though she might be feeling defensive.

4. **Man:** He talks about how he feels, using "I" language.

5. **Woman:** No comment.

6. **Man:** He expresses his feelings in "I" language.

7. **Woman:** She's speaking sarcastically, indicating defensiveness.

8. **Man:** He states his interpretation of her feelings and asks her to confirm or deny — good "I" language.

9. **Woman:** She's still speaking defensively.

10. **Man:** He's expressing his primary feelings of hurt in "I" language. Because of her defensiveness, he is taking an emotional risk in doing so.

11. **Woman:** She's making accusations and speaking defensively.

12. **Man:** He's expressing his primary feelings in "I" language. He's also avoiding defensiveness.

13. **Woman:** She's now taking the risk of expressing her primary feelings of fear, using "I" language.

Part A.

Study the sample conversation below, and indicate those statements you feel show vulnerability.

1. **Man:** How are the kids today?

2. **Woman:** Well, they're fine, but I'd like to discuss them with you. Something's been bothering me.

3. **Man:** What's that? Anybody in trouble?

4. **Woman:** No, they've been asking a lot about you lately, since you've been away so much. They miss you, and they ask me why Daddy doesn't play with them anymore.

5. **Man:** Daddy doesn't play with them because Daddy's out earning their meals and the roof over their heads. Not to mention all the toys and goodies I buy them. Don't they appreciate anything?

6. **Woman:** Well, I do explain to them how busy you are, but they still miss playing with you. They like you better than toys.

7. **Man:** Are you telling me I neglect my children? After I work 50 to 60 hours a week...

8. **Woman:** No, I'm not trying to tell you that. I wanted you to be aware of how they were feeling, because I assumed you'd want to know.

9. **Man:** I'm sorry. I do want to know. It's just that sometimes I feel really guilty about not spending more time with our children. I'm so busy and so tired.

10. **Woman:** I understand that, and I'm willing to help you find a way to solve the problem.

11. **Man:** Well, I'd like them to feel sure that I love them.

Part B.

For each statement you indicated, write why you think it shows vulnerability.

1. Man: _____
   _____

2. Woman: _____
   _____

3. Man: _____
   _____

4. Woman: _____
   _____

5. Man: _____
   _____

6. Woman: _____
   _____

7. Man: _____
   _____

8. Woman: _____
   _____

9. Man: _____
   _____

10. Woman: _____
    _____

11. Man: _____
    _____

Part A.

Below, we have indicated those statements we feel show vulnerability.

1. **Man:** How are the kids today?

2. **Woman:** *Well, they're fine, but I'd like to discuss them with you. Something's been bothering me.*

3. **Man:** What's that? Anybody in trouble?

4. **Woman:** No, they've been asking a lot about you lately, since you've been away so much. They miss you, and they ask me why Daddy doesn't play with them anymore.

5. **Man:** Daddy doesn't play with them because Daddy's out earning their meals and the roof over their heads. Not to mention all the toys and goodies I buy them. Don't they appreciate anything?

6. **Woman:** Well, I do explain to them how busy you are, but they still miss playing with you. They like you better than toys.

7. **Man:** Are you telling me I neglect my children? After I work 50 to 60 hours a week...

8. **Woman:** *No, I'm not trying to tell you that. I wanted you to be aware of how they were feeling, because I assumed you'd want to know.*

9. **Man:** *I'm sorry. I do want to know. It's just that sometimes I feel really guilty about not spending more time with our children. I'm so busy and so tired.*

10. **Woman:** *I understand that, and I'm willing to help you find a way to solve the problem.*

11. **Man:** *Well, I'd like them to feel sure that I love them.*

Part B.

For each statement we indicated, we've shown why we think it shows vulnerability.

1. **Man:** No comment.

2. **Woman:** You could have underlined these statements if you assumed she was bringing up a touchy subject and, therefore, taking an emotional risk.

3. **Man:** No comment.

4. **Woman:** She uses "I" language to state the problem.

5. **Man:** He's beginning to sound defensive.

6. **Woman:** She tries to clarify her meaning, using "I" language.

7. **Man:** He's speaking defensively.

8. **Woman:** She is taking an emotional risk and avoiding defensiveness herself.

9. **Man:** He is overcoming his defensiveness to risk expressing his primary feelings in "I" language.

10. **Woman:** You may or may not have underlined this statement. She's expressing primary feelings in "I" language.

11. **Man:** He is expressing primary feelings in "I" language. Given his earlier sensitivity, this probably represents an emotional risk for him.

CHAPTER **8**

EFFECTIVE PERSONAL EXPRESSION

INTRODUCTION

T O THIS point, you have learned quite a number of skills. You've learned to:

- Identify self-responsibility.
- Explore the scope of your feelings.
- Identify the sequence of your feelings.
- Deal more constructively with anger.
- Identify and use "I" language.
- Identify defensiveness.
- Identify vulnerability.

In this chapter, you'll be using all of these skills to identify effective personal expression. After all, the goal of this volume has been to get you started in expressing yourself more effectively with your partner. The benefits of such improvement in your communication skills should be obvious. In this chapter, you'll be taking your first steps toward this goal.

GOAL

Given a conversation between partners, you will be asked to identify instances of ineffective personal expression and to explain your answers.

Effective personal expression is achieved when you are:

1. Using "I" language.

2. Expressing primary feelings.

3. Exercising self-responsibility.

 ELABORATION

Recognizing effective personal expression in a written conversation will require some use of your own common sense and judgment because the characteristics are not always easy to observe. Below, the three characteristics are explained in terms of what *can* be observed in a written conversation.

1. Using "I" Language

You have already learned to identify the use or nonuse of "I" language in Chapter Five. It is the easiest of the characteristics to observe and, therefore, it is usually the key factor in identifying weaknesses in effective personal expression. Remember that an individual using "I" language:

a. Starts every sentence about feelings with "I."

b. Uses verbs that imply "want" rather than "should" or "ought."

c. Asks "what" rather than asking for justification or "why."

d. Makes his or her feelings or concerns known before asking a question.

e. Talks about how another person is feeling or behaving now rather than generalizing about the past or predicting the future.

f. Makes every effort to be aware of and express what he or she feels rather than saying, "I don't know."

You may want to quickly review Chapter Five before beginning the sample conversations in this chapter.

2. Expressing Primary Feelings

You learned about primary and secondary feelings in Chapter Three. You recall that:

Primary Feelings include fear, frustration, emotional hurt, and physical pain. These feelings usually occur most immediately in an emotional situation.

192

They are not usually destructive or coercive and can be readily expressed and dealt with by most people. When you are aware of and can identify your primary feelings, you are better able to act in your own best interest.

Secondary Feelings include anger, resentment, and hostility, and are those feelings that may occur immediately after primary feelings. They are often so powerful and coercive that they can conceal primary feelings. These feelings often result in destructive communication and are very difficult for most people to deal with directly. When you are experiencing secondary feelings, very often you will be unable to act in your best interest.

The point to be made here is that the goal of effective personal expression is to express primary feelings. This is not to say that secondary feelings have no place. If you are feeling angry or jealous, it is acceptable to say, "I'm angry," or "I'm jealous." But once these feelings are out, it is most important to work back to your primary feelings — what you are angry or jealous about. You may be angry because you are hurt. It is only when secondary feelings completely take over and an individual is no longer working back to primary feelings that personal expression becomes ineffective. Observing this in a written, or even a spoken, conversation is a bit more difficult than listening for "I" language. What is usually noticeable is that as the conversation goes on, an individual seems to have lost control and is expressing only secondary feelings. You may observe that the individual has been behaving defensively for a better part of the conversation. As we mentioned earlier, this is where your judgment comes in. You may want to review Chapter Three before going on to the sample conversations in this chapter.

3. **Exercising Self-Responsibility**

You learned about self-responsibility in the first chapter of this book. As you recall, you are exercising self-responsibility when you:

a. Act in your own best interest, having considered:

   (1) Your wants and goals.

   (2) The long- and short-term results of your actions.

   (3) The possible effects of your actions on those you care about.

b. Communicate your intentions and feelings.

c. Do NOT blame others or hold them responsible for your behavior.

In a written conversation, it's hard to know if an individual is acting in his or her own best interest. There are, however, some remarks that can alert you. You may notice that an individual asks or talks only about what the other person wants and expresses no personal preferences. For instance, that individual might make guesses or projections about the other's desires. "I suppose you'd like to go out to dinner tonight," is an example. Usually you will already have identified such instances as not being "I" language. "I don't know" or "I don't care" are statements that indicate a lack of self-responsibility. So are remarks made by one individual blaming another for his feelings or actions. Before going on to the sample conversations, you may want to review Chapter One.

SAMPLE
CONVERSATIONS

FOLLOWING ARE five sample conversations in which instances of ineffective personal expression are indicated. The commentary presents remarks for each statement. Read only as many samples as you need to be able to identify instances of ineffective expression on your own.

NOTE:

We would like to remind you that, outside of this workbook, the skills you learn in this chapter need to be applied to your own behavior. Although you may monitor your partner's behavior, we suggest that you refrain from criticizing. For instance, if your partner is not using "I" language, express your desire to hear "I" language rather than criticizing him or her for not using it.

Sample Conversation 1

Indicated below in bold italics are those statements or phrases that represent ineffective personal expression. See the commentary for further explanation.

COMMENTARY

Man: I'm going to take the boys down to the park to practice baseball today. How does that fit into your schedule?

He states his intentions and then asks a question — good "I" language.

Woman: *Just great. I'll just do all the things I planned for us by myself — as usual.*

She is not expressing primary feelings. She is using some "I" language, but her tone is sarcastic and possibly defensive.

Man: I didn't know you had plans for us.

No comment.

Woman: *I'm not surprised. You never think about planning anything with me. You spend all your free time with the kids.*

More sarcasm. Also she is not using "I" language — she is generalizing about his behavior, using "you."

Man: *What a martyr! You're not half as neglected as you think you are.*

He is not using "I" language. He may be feeling defensive since he is making accusations.

Woman: *How would you know? You're never around to find out.*

She is still sarcastic and still not expressing primary feelings using "I" language. Note her use of "never."

Man: *Don't you think it's important for me to spend time with our kids?*

He asks a question that actually expresses his opinion, rather than stating his opinion and then asking what she thinks.

Woman: *Sure, but you seem to enjoy their company a lot more than mine. You guys go out and have fun and I just sit at home.*

She is making assumptions about his preferences without asking him. She is probably feeling defensive.

Man: I'd love for you to come along. I never thought you'd want to.

He uses "I" language to talk about his wants.

Woman: Well, I do want to. I like seeing the kids have fun with their father, and I'm hurt that I haven't been asked to join.

She uses "I" language to talk about her desires and feelings.

196

The conversation below is similar to the previous one, except that below the individuals are expressing themselves more effectively. Notice how the overall tone differs.

Man: I'm going to take the boys down to the park to practice baseball today. How does that fit into your schedule?

Woman: I had hoped we could do something together.

Man: Oh, I didn't realize that.

Woman: I know you like to spend a lot of your free time with the kids, but I'd like to get in on some of it myself. I feel left out sitting at home while you guys are out having so much fun.

Man: I'd love for you to come along with us. How do you feel about that?

Woman: I'd like that. I like seeing the children having fun with you. I'd like to do something with you alone later too.

Man: I'd like that too.

Sample Conversation 2

Indicated below in bold italics are those statements or phrases that represent ineffective personal expression. See the commentary for further explanation.

COMMENTARY

Man: ***Well, it's about time you came home. You might be interested to know that your children are starving.***

He begins the conversation with a sarcastic accusation. He is not expressing primary feelings or using "I" language.

Woman: I was working late. I wanted to get some things finished before the weekend. I get the distinct feeling that you're annoyed with me.

She expresses her concern that he is annoyed, leaving him free to confirm or deny.

Man: I am very annoyed. These kids have been pestering me for the last hour about when we're going to eat.

He uses "I" language to express his feelings.

Woman: Did you feed them?

No comment.

Man: No, I didn't. ***How was I supposed to know you were going to be late? Besides, it's not my responsibility.***

He asks a question that masks his opinion. Also, he's blaming her for his annoyance.

Woman: I'd like to discuss that issue with you later on. Right now I'm going to get some dinner ready for us.

She uses "I" language to express her feelings and intentions.

Man: ***I suppose a late supper is better than no supper.***

More sarcasm. He has slipped back into expressing only secondary feelings.

Woman: Next time I'll call when I'm going to be late so you'll know. I can see that caused a problem for you tonight.

She uses "I" language to express her feelings and intentions.

Man: ***The problem is that you should be here to fix dinner. It's your responsibility, not mine.***

He is not using "I" language because he is sending a "you" message about what she ought to do. He is also blaming her for not being there, indicating a lack of self-responsibility on his part.

198

The conversation below is similar to the previous one, except that below the individuals are expressing themselves more effectively. Notice how the overall tone differs.

Man: Hi. I wasn't expecting you so late. The children are starving.

Woman: I was working late. I wanted to get some things finished before the weekend. I get the feeling you're annoyed with me.

Man: Well, I am kind of frustrated. These kids have been pestering me for the last hour about when we're going to eat.

Woman: Did you feed them?

Man: No, I didn't. I kept thinking you'd be home any minute. I wasn't really prepared to feed them.

Woman: I'd like to talk with you more about that later. Right now I'm going to get some dinner ready. I'll try to call next time. I can see it caused a problem for you.

Man: I'd appreciate that.

Sample Conversation 3

Indicated below are those statements or phrases that represent ineffective personal expression. See the commentary for further explanation.

COMMENTARY

Woman: *What exactly did you mean last night when you said I wasn't a very interesting sexual partner?*

She begins the conversation with a question without stating her concerns. She also says "you said," which is not "I" language.

Man: *Well, you never do anything anymore but lie there. I have to do everything.*

He sends a "you" message generalizing about her behavior. He also talks about what he "has to" do.

Woman: *What "everything?" You just hop on and hop off and that's supposed to be interesting? You used to do more than that.*

She is being sarcastic and sending a lot of "you" messages.

Man: *Maybe so, but you take so long to get warmed up it isn't worth it. It's a lot of work.*

He's sending "you" messages. He has yet to express any primary feelings.

Woman: *That depends on how you look at it. You ejaculate so fast, no woman could keep up with you.*

She's still sending "you" messages and has not expressed any primary feelings.

Man: I don't think five minutes is fast. *And anyway, we've had sex so infrequently lately. Only once a month.*

His use of "we" is not "I" language.

Woman: *That's a likely excuse — it's not just once a month. It's at least once a week.*

She uses more sarcasm.

Man: *Who are you having intercourse with?*

He asks a question that barely conceals a sarcastic opinion.

Woman: I think our sexual relationship needs some help, and *every time* I try to talk about it seriously, *you find a way to avoid dealing with it.*

She is attempting to state the problem, but she generalizes about the situation with "every time" and sends a "you" message.

Man: *You're the one who needs help.*

He sends a "you" message that probably indicates defensiveness.

Woman: I can't fix this problem by myself, and my gynecologist has been no help. I really don't know where to go from here.

She uses "I" language to talk about her feelings.

The conversation below is similar to the previous one, except that below the individuals are expressing themselves more effectively. Notice how the overall tone differs.

Woman: Last night when we were talking, I understood you to say that I wasn't a very interesting sexual partner. I was hurt by that and I'd like to know if I understood you correctly.

Man: Well, what I meant was that I feel like I have to do everything. I feel pressured to perform for you.

Woman: It takes me a while to get warmed up, and by the time I do, you've already ejaculated. I feel like I can't keep up with you.

Man: I would be willing to slow down, except that then I have a hard time keeping myself stimulated. I'd like some help from you in that respect. In fact, I guess that's what I meant last night. I'd like for you to participate more. I think that would make it more exciting and interesting for me. Maybe for you too. How do you feel about that?

Woman: I'd like to give it a try.

Indicated below are those statements or phrases that represent ineffective personal expression. See the commentary for further explanation.

COMMENTARY

Man: *You know, you've really got it made!*

He begins the conversation in an irritated tone of voice and is not using "I" language. He has not expressed his primary feelings.

Woman: I don't understand what you mean.

She is confused by his statement.

Man: *You not only got the pool you wanted, you got someone to take care of it for you too.*

Still no primary feelings. He is sending out "you" messages.

Woman: I get the feeling you're upset that I don't clean the pool. Is that it?

She states her feelings before asking a question — good "I" language.

Man: *That's it, all right. You never lift a finger to vacuum it, or even skim the leaves. You just expect me to do it. I suppose you think it's a man's job.*

He generalizes about her behavior and makes assumptions about what she thinks. He is sounding rather defensive.

Woman: I don't remember you complaining before now; and to tell you the truth, I have just expected you to do it. *I'll take care of it myself if that's what you want.*

She may be reflecting a lack of self-responsibility by this last statement.

Man: Well, I don't know if that's fair. After all, I do swim too. I just get resentful sometimes, because I feel I'm totally responsible. I don't find the maintenance part fun and, naturally, I'd like to get out of at least some of the dirty work.

He uses "I" language to talk about his desires and feelings.

Woman: I'd be willing then to work out some sort of division of chores or a schedule. I enjoy swimming enough that it's worth my effort.

She uses "I" language to talk about her desires and feelings.

The conversation below is similar to the previous one, except that below the individuals are expressing themselves more effectively. Notice how the overall tone differs.

Man: I am getting really frustrated about cleaning the pool. I don't like to do it, and I'd really like to have some help.

Woman: I didn't realize it bothered you so much. I'll be glad to help take care of it. I know it's an unpleasant job.

Man: I'd really appreciate that. I was beginning to get very irritated and I wanted to avoid that. I guess I could have had your help a long time ago.

Woman: Well, I enjoy swimming enough that it's certainly worth my effort.

Indicated below are those statements or phrases that represent ineffective personal expression. See the commentary for further explanation.

COMMENTARY

Man: *What's the matter?*

He asks a question without stating his concerns first.

Woman: I've been doing housework all day, and *there you sit watching TV.*

She sends a sarcastic or irritated "you" message about his behavior.

Man: So?

He's confused about her meaning.

Woman: So, I'd like to do something fun after working all day.

She states her desires in "I" language.

Man: Fine, but *how can you possibly spend a whole day doing housework?*

He asks a "why" question that masks his criticism of her.

Woman: Well, *you just try it some time. It's not as easy as you think.*

She sends "you" messages.

Man: I could probably do it in 30 minutes — or maybe an hour at the most. *You waste too much time making things perfect.*

He sends a "you" message.

Woman: *You know, it's really tiresome to have you come home and tell me I've wasted the whole day when I know that if things weren't just right, you'd complain.*

She sounds as though she is trying to express her primary feelings, but she is not using "I" language.

Man: I guess I just don't have any concept of what it takes to get this house in order.

He expresses his feelings in "I" language.

Woman: I appreciate hearing that. What I don't like is hearing that I wasted my whole day. I feel hurt and stupid when you say I'm wasting my time. I'd feel much happier if you believed I knew what I was doing.

She uses "I" language to talk about her feelings and desires.

Effective Expression

The conversation below is similar to the previous one, except that below the individuals are expressing themselves more effectively. Notice how the overall tone differs.

Man: I get the feeling that all is not well with you. Is there a problem?

Woman: I've been doing housework all day, and I'd like to have some attention and sympathy.

Man: Would you like to watch TV with me?

Woman: For a while, but I really want to do something fun after all that work I did today.

Man: I guess I don't have any concept of what it takes to get the house in order. It's difficult for me to appreciate that.

Woman: I can understand that.

Man: I am willing to do something fun with you tonight.

PRACTICE

FOLLOWING ARE five practice items similar to the conversations in the sample conversation section. You are to indicate those statements you feel reflect ineffective expression. On the next page, you are to give your reasons in the blanks provided. Make your comments brief, like those in the commentaries in the sample conversation section. Look at the feedback for each item after completing the item. If you feel you've done the first couple of items well, you may consider yourself finished with the instructional part of this book. If you have any trouble with the practice, go back and review the definition, the elaboration, and the sample conversations. Then try the practice again.

PRACTICE 1

Part A.

Indicate those statements or phrases you feel represent ineffective personal expression.

1. **Man:** Don't you think our daughter's a little young to be dating already? I can't believe you let her stay out so late last night.

2. **Woman:** One o'clock isn't so late. You're being overprotective.

3. **Man:** Well, I call it parental responsibility, and I certainly think you ought to be taking this a lot more seriously.

4. **Woman:** I see — so I'm an irresponsible mother. Frankly, I'd say you are becoming a little narrow-minded in your old age. You didn't think I was too young when you were dating me.

5. **Man:** You were 17. She's only 15.

6. **Woman:** I know she's younger, but I feel that she is mature enough to take care of herself. She and I have had long talks lately about her dating, and she's conducted herself very well. I trust her judgment.

7. **Man:** How can you be so callous, though? Don't you worry even a little?

8. **Woman:** Of course I worry. I get really scared sometimes, but I'm not going to cut off her freedom just to make myself feel better.

9. **Man:** Maybe I'll talk to her myself—tell her how I feel. I worry about her a lot, and I guess I just get carried away.

Part B.

For each statement or phrase you indicated on the facing page, use the space below to explain briefly why you feel the statement represents ineffective personal expression.

1. Man: _____

_____

2. Woman: _____

_____

3. Man: _____

_____

4. Woman: _____

_____

5. Man: _____

_____

6. Woman: _____

_____

7. Man: _____

_____

8. Woman: _____

_____

9. Man: _____

_____

FEEDBACK 1

Part A.

Below, we have indicated in bold italics those statements or phrases we feel represent ineffective personal expression.

1. **Man:** ***Don't you think our daughter's a little young to be dating already? I can't believe you let her stay out so late last night.***

2. **Woman:** ***One o'clock isn't so late. You're being overprotective.***

3. **Man:** Well, I call it parental responsibility, and ***I certainly think you ought to be taking this a lot more seriously.***

4. **Woman:** I see — ***so I'm an irresponsible mother.*** Frankly, I'd say ***you are becoming a little narrow-minded in your old age. You didn't think I was too young when you were dating me.***

5. **Man:** You were 17. She's only 15.

6. **Woman:** I know she's younger, but I feel that she is mature enough to take care of herself. She and I have had long talks lately about her dating, and she's conducted herself very well. I trust her judgment.

7. **Man:** ***How can you be so callous, though? Don't you worry even a little?***

8. **Woman:** Of course I worry. I get really scared sometimes, but I'm not going to cut off her freedom just to make myself feel better.

9. **Man:** Maybe I'll talk to her myself — tell her how I feel. I worry about her a lot, and I guess I just get carried away.

Part B.

Below, you'll find an explanation for each of the statements or phrases we indicated on the facing page. Your explanations will probably be a little different.

1. **Man:** He opens the conversation with a question that barely conceals his opinion. The following statement sounds like an accusation.

2. **Woman:** She isn't using "I" language. The second remark is a "you" message.

3. **Man:** He sends a "you" message telling her what she "ought" to do.

4. **Woman:** She is sounding defensive here. She sends out a couple of "you" messages. To this point, she hasn't expressed any primary feelings.

5. **Man:** No comment.

6. **Woman:** She uses "I" language to talk about her feelings and experience.

7. **Man:** He's asking a question that really expresses his opinion that she is callous and never worries. He is not using "I" language and, to this point, hasn't expressed any primary feelings.

8. **Woman:** She talks about her fears, using "I" language.

9. **Man:** He expresses his fears, using "I" language.

Part A.

Indicate those statements or phrases you feel represent ineffective personal expression.

1. **Woman:** Aren't we ever going to clean the garage?

2. **Man:** Maybe, maybe not.

3. **Woman:** Oh come on, you know it has to be cleaned.

4. **Man:** Frankly, I'm not bothered by it and I don't know why you are.

5. **Woman:** Because I have such a hard time finding things and when I do, they're filthy dirty.

6. **Man:** Why don't you clean it yourself?

7. **Woman:** Because it's your responsibility too!

8. **Man:** Well, you're barking up the wrong tree if you expect me to go for that logic. I resent feeling like I'm being talked into doing something I don't want to do. I get stubborn.

9. **Woman:** Yes, I can see that. I guess what frustrates me is that I really do want to clean the garage, but I don't know how to get it done. I'm afraid to move any of your stuff because I've done that in the past and you've complained about not being able to find anything.

10. **Man:** I see. If that's the problem, I'd feel a lot more willing to help work something out.

Part B.

For each statement or phrase you indicated on the facing page, use the space below to explain briefly why you feel the statement represents ineffective personal expression.

1. **Woman:** _____

2. **Man:** _____

3. **Woman:** _____

4. **Man:** _____

5. **Woman:** _____

6. **Man:** _____

7. **Woman:** _____

8. **Man:** _____

9. **Woman:** _____

10. **Man:** _____

FEEDBACK 2

Part A.

Below, we have indicated in bold italics those statements or phrases we feel represent ineffective personal expression.

1. **Woman:** ***Aren't we ever going to clean the garage?***

2. **Man:** Maybe, maybe not.

3. **Woman:** ***Oh come on, you know it has to be cleaned.***

4. **Man:** Frankly, I'm not bothered by it and I don't know ***why you are.***

5. **Woman:** Because I have such a hard time finding things and when I do, they're filthy dirty.

6. **Man:** ***Why don't you clean it yourself?***

7. **Woman:** ***Because it's your responsibility too!***

8. **Man:** ***Well, you're barking up the wrong tree if you expect me to go for that logic.*** I resent feeling like I'm being talked into doing something I don't want to do. I get stubborn.

9. **Woman:** Yes, I can see that. I guess what frustrates me is that I really do want to clean the garage, but I don't know how to get it done. I'm afraid to move any of your stuff because I've done that in the past and you've complained about not being able to find anything.

10. **Man:** I see. If that's the problem, I'd feel a lot more willing to help work something out.

Part B.

Below, you'll find an explanation for each of the statements or phrases we indicated on the facing page. Your explanations will probably be a little different.

1. **Woman:** She begins the conversation not using "I" language. She's asked a question without stating her concerns, but her opinion is obvious.

2. **Man:** He probably feels trapped by her question.

3. **Woman:** She sends a "you" message telling him about his obligation.

4. **Man:** The "why" here is not "I" language. It doesn't matter why.

5. **Woman:** No comment.

6. **Man:** This question is not "I" language. He asks a question that is really meant to express his opinion.

7. **Woman:** Again, she sends a "you" message about his obligations. This remark indicates a lack of self-responsibility.

8. **Man:** He begins with a "you" message. To this point, he hasn't really expressed any primary feelings.

9. **Woman:** She uses "I" language to talk about her feelings and desires.

10. **Man:** He uses "I" language to talk about his feelings.

PRACTICE 3

Part A.

Indicate those statements or phrases you feel represent ineffective personal expression.

1. **Man:** I get the feeling you're a little down. Is something wrong?

2. **Woman:** I'm tired of having to make all the decisions about everything all by myself. You're never home to help me out.

3. **Man:** I see. You're upset about how much time I spend at work. Is that it?

4. **Woman:** Yes, I don't know why you can't work 8 to 5 like other men.

5. **Man:** I work as much as I do because I feel it's important to my career — especially right now.

6. **Woman:** Oh, and my needs just don't count, I suppose.

7. **Man:** Yes, they do. I thought we had come to an agreement about me spending more time with you. I agreed to try to spend both days each weekend at home, and I thought you agreed too.

8. **Woman:** Only because I knew that was the best I could get.

9. **Man:** I see, and now you're not satisfied. Is that right?

10. **Woman:** No, I'm not satisfied.

11. **Man:** Well, I thought I was doing what you wanted all this time. I'd like to know what you really want because I'd like to work this out so that I'm happy and you're happy.

Part B.

For each statement or phrase you indicated on the facing page, use the space below to explain briefly why you feel the statement represents ineffective personal expression.

1. **Man:** _____

_____

2. **Woman:** _____

_____

3. **Man:** _____

_____

4. **Woman:** _____

_____

5. **Man:** _____

_____

6. **Woman:** _____

_____

7. **Man:** _____

_____

8. **Woman:** _____

_____

9. **Man:** _____

_____

10. **Woman:** _____

_____

11. **Man:** _____

_____

FEEDBACK 3

Part A.

Below, we have indicated those statements or phrases we feel represent ineffective personal expression.

1. **Man:** I get the feeling you're a little down. Is something wrong?

2. **Woman:** *I'm tired of having to make all the decisions about everything by myself. You're never home to help me out.*

3. **Man:** I see. You're upset about how much time I spend at work. Is that it?

4. **Woman:** Yes, I don't know *why you can't* work 8 to 5 like other men.

5. **Man:** I work as much as I do because I feel it's important to my career — especially right now.

6. **Woman:** Oh, and *my needs just don't count, I suppose.*

7. **Man:** Yes, they do. I thought we had come to an agreement about me spending more time with you. I agreed to try to spend both days each weekend at home, and I thought you agreed too.

8. **Woman:** *Only because I knew that was the best I could get.*

9. **Man:** I see, and now you're not satisfied. Is that right?

10. **Woman:** No, I'm not satisfied.

11. **Man:** Well, I thought I was doing what you wanted all this time. I'd like to know what you really want because I'd like to work this out so that I'm happy and you're happy.

218

Part B.

Below, you'll find an explanation for each of the statements or phrases we indicated on the facing page. Your explanations will probably be a little different.

1. **Man:** He states his concerns before asking a question — good "I" language.

2. **Woman:** She is not using "I" language. She implies that he has a duty and generalizes by using "all," "everything," "all by myself," and "never." She sounds like she's blaming him for her problem, indicating a lack of self-responsibility.

3. **Man:** Again, he states his feelings before asking a question — good "I" language.

4. **Woman:** The "why" here is not "I" language.

5. **Man:** He uses "I" language to express his feelings and desires.

6. **Woman:** She sounds defensive. She's assuming her needs don't count, but he hasn't said that.

7. **Man:** He's using "I" language.

8. **Woman:** This statement reflects a lack of self-responsibility. She is probably speaking sarcastically.

9. **Man:** He states his feelings before asking a question — good "I" language.

10. **Woman:** She expresses her feelings in "I" language.

11. **Man:** He continues to use "I" language.

PRACTICE 4

Part A.

Indicate those statements or phrases you feel represent ineffective personal expression.

1. **Woman:** I am dying to get out of the house. Could we please do something tonight?

2. **Man:** Sure, anything you want.

3. **Woman:** Doesn't matter to me, just so long as it's out.

4. **Man:** Well, you must have some preferences.

5. **Woman:** No, I'll go anywhere you want.

6. **Man:** You like to dance. How about if we go dancing?

7. **Woman:** We always go dancing when we go out.

8. **Man:** I thought you liked it.

9. **Woman:** I do, but not all the time.

10. **Man:** Then, what would you like to do?

11. **Woman:** I'd like to hear some live entertainment where there's no dancing.

12. **Man:** Hey, I like that idea too. I prefer folk-type music. What about you?

Part B.

For each statement or phrase you indicated on the facing page, use the space below to explain briefly why you feel the statement represents ineffective personal expression.

1. Woman: _____

_____

2. Man: _____

_____

3. Woman: _____

_____

4. Man: _____

_____

5. Woman: _____

_____

6. Man: _____

_____

7. Woman: _____

_____

8. Man: _____

_____

9. Woman: _____

_____

10. Man: _____

_____

11. Woman: _____

_____

12. Man: _____

_____

Part A.

Below, we have indicated those statements or phrases we feel represent ineffective personal expression.

1. **Woman:** I am dying to get out of the house. Could we please do something tonight?

2. **Man:** Sure, *anything you want.*

3. **Woman:** *Doesn't matter to me, just so long as it's out.*

4. **Man:** Well, *you must have* some preferences.

5. **Woman:** *No, I'll go anywhere you want.*

6. **Man:** *You like to dance. How about if we go dancing?*

7. **Woman:** *We always go dancing when we go out.*

8. **Man:** I thought you liked it.

9. **Woman:** I do, but not *all the time.*

10. **Man:** *Then, what would you like to do?*

11. **Woman:** I'd like to hear some live entertainment where there's no dancing.

12. **Man:** Hey, I like that idea too. I prefer folk-type music. What about you?

Part B.

Below, you'll find an explanation for each of the statements or phrases we indicated on the facing page. Your explanations will probably be a little different.

1. **Woman:** She uses "we" — not "I" language.

2. **Man:** By saying "anything you want," he is not using "I" language and shows a lack of self-responsibility.

3. **Woman:** In essence, she is saying she doesn't care. She is not using "I" language or exercising self-responsibility.

4. **Man:** "You must" is not "I" language. To this point, he hasn't expressed any preferences or primary feelings.

5. **Woman:** She is still not exercising self-responsibility. Nor has she expressed any primary feelings.

6. **Man:** He's using "you" and "we" and not really stating his preferences.

7. **Woman:** She generalizes by saying "we always" — not "I" language.

8. **Man:** No comment.

9. **Woman:** She generalizes again with "all the time." Don't be concerned if you missed this one.

10. **Man:** He fails to state his preferences.

11. **Woman:** She finally says what she wants, using "I" language.

12. **Man:** He finally says what he wants, using "I" language.

PRACTICE 5

Part A.

Indicate those statements or phrases you feel represent ineffective personal expression.

1. **Man:** I was very embarrassed at the Nelson's party last night. I wondered if we could talk about it.

2. **Woman:** Okay. I didn't realize you were embarrassed. What was it about?

3. **Man:** Your flirting with Harry. It was so obvious, you made a fool of me and of yourself.

4. **Woman:** I'm sorry you feel that way, but I was enjoying myself and I don't regret my behavior.

5. **Man:** And you don't care how it made me look, do you? You just wanted to lap up all that attention.

6. **Woman:** I find Harry to be an interesting person. I was talking to him because of that, not because I craved attention. And I do care that you're bothered.

7. **Man:** But you'd do it again, wouldn't you?

8. **Woman:** If I felt like it. I feel good about getting a chance to interact with other people.

9. **Man:** Because I'm not enough for you. Is that it?

10. **Woman:** No, that is not it. I'd like to discuss this at another time. I'm beginning to feel very defensive.

11. **Man:** You said you wanted to talk about it.

12. **Woman:** I changed my mind. I feel too defensive.

Part B.

For each statement or phrase you indicated on the facing page, use the space below to explain briefly why you feel the statement represents ineffective personal expression.

1. Woman: _____

_____

2. Man: _____

_____

3. Woman: _____

_____

4. Man: _____

_____

5. Woman: _____

_____

6. Man: _____

_____

7. Woman: _____

_____

8. Man: _____

_____

9. Woman: _____

_____

10. Man: _____

_____

11. Woman: _____

_____

12. Man: _____

_____

FEEDBACK 5

Part A.

Below, we have indicated those statements or phrases we feel represent ineffective personal expression.

1. **Man:** I was very embarrassed at the Nelson's party last night. I wondered if we could talk about it.

2. **Woman:** Okay. I didn't realize you were embarrassed. What was it about?

3. **Man:** *Your flirting with Harry. It was so obvious, you made a fool of me and of yourself.*

4. **Woman:** I'm sorry you feel that way, but I was enjoying myself and *I don't regret my behavior.*

5. **Man:** *And you don't care how it made me look, do you? You just wanted to lap up all that attention.*

6. **Woman:** I find Harry to be an interesting person. I was talking to him because of that, not because I craved attention. And I do care that you're bothered.

7. **Man:** But *you'd do it again, wouldn't you?*

8. **Woman:** *If I felt like it.* I feel good about getting a chance to interact with other people.

9. **Man:** *Because I'm not enough for you. Is that it?*

10. **Woman:** No, that is not it. I'd like to discuss this at another time. I'm beginning to feel very defensive.

11. **Man:** *You said you wanted to talk about it.*

12. **Woman:** I changed my mind. I feel too defensive.

Part B.

Below, you'll find an explanation for each of the statements or phrases we indicated on the facing page. Your explanations will probably be a little different.

1. **Man:** He uses "I" language to express his feelings and desires.

2. **Woman:** No comment.

3. **Man:** He accuses her of flirting, indicating possible defensiveness. He is not using "I" language.

4. **Woman:** She indicates a possible lack of self-responsibility by not considering the effects of her actions on him. Don't be concerned if you missed this one.

5. **Man:** He accuses her of not caring. He is not using "I" language, nor is he expressing any primary feelings.

6. **Woman:** She uses "I" language to talk about her feelings.

7. **Man:** Defensiveness is indicated by his continuing accusations and nonuse of "I" language.

8. **Woman:** Again, she doesn't seem to be considering his feelings very carefully, indicating a lack of self-responsibility. Don't be concerned if you missed this one.

9. **Man:** He is still making defensive accusations. Except for his opening statement, he hasn't expressed any primary feelings.

10. **Woman:** She uses "I" language to express her discomfort.

11. **Man:** He's not using "I" language — "you said you."

12. **Woman:** She's still using "I" language.

EPILOGUE

Now What?

Now that you've completed this workbook you're probably wondering what comes next. You may have already experienced some problems in using the skills you've been developing. Don't be discouraged if you can't seem to do it all right away. You've learned a lot here and you will learn even more as you practice your skills. Have patience with yourself but be persistent. You will find that even more can be gotten out of this text when you reread parts of it. When you find yourself questioning or confused about something you've learned, we suggest that you reread the chapter or chapters dealing with that topic. They will give you new insights based on your new experiences.

"I" Language: A Little At A Time

Many people find it difficult to learn "I" language all at once. Not surprising. It's difficult to change the way you express yourself. We recommend that you not attempt all six rules of "I" language right away. Take a few at a time and build. Here's the progression we recommend.

1. Begin with the first two rules for using "I" language. Concentrate on:

   a. Starting every sentence about feelings with "I."

   b. Using verbs that imply "want" rather than "should."

Work with these skills for one week or until you feel comfortable with them.

2. Next, work on your question-asking habits. Concentrate on:

   a. Making your feelings or concerns known before asking questions rather than hiding opinions behind questions.

   b. Asking "what" rather than "why" when asking about feelings.

Concentrate on building these habits for the next week but don't forget the first two. Keep using "I" and avoiding "shoulds" and "oughts."

3. Now, you're ready to work on the last two. Concentrate on:

   a. Speaking only about how a person is feeling or behaving *now* rather than generalizing about the past or predicting the future.

   b. Being conscientious about expressing what you *do* know about your feelings rather than saying "I don't know."

Again, work with these skills for about one week but don't forget the first four.

As you begin work on each new skill, reread the portion of Chapter 5 that deals with that skill. Building gradually and cumulatively will help you work these new skills into your everyday language. You will feel more and more confident in your skill and more comfortable as time goes on.

Points To Remember

This is a good place to remind you of some issues critical to the success of the skills taught in this book.

ONE: What you've learned here is meant to be used with people you love and trust. If basic love and trust don't exist between individuals, the use of "I" language or any of the other concepts in this book will probably not bring you closer together or heal a troubled relationship.

TWO: Everything you've learned from this book is meant for your personal use. It is *not* something you do to or for someone else. Our purpose is to help you change *your* behavior, not help you change somebody else's.

You may wish to encourage others you care about to learn the skills you've learned here. This enthusiasm is understandable, but avoid the temptation to crusade. Trying to convert or correct people will only create resistance. Nobody likes a "goody two shoes" or a "holier than thou" attitude. Setting an example is a lot more effective and less obnoxious.

THREE: The skills taught here are meant to be used as tools to help you communicate better. But, effective tools can also be effective weapons. It's all in your attitude. Used with a destructive attitude your skills will almost certainly have a destructive effect on your relationships.

Finally, no single tool works all of the time. Don't make the mistake of building the concepts in this book into a rigid belief system. In other words, be flexible. What you've learned should never be allowed to spoil moments of fun or intimacy. Be guided by this book; don't let it run your life.